Vernon Watkins

on

Dylan Thomas

and other poets and poetry

Vernon Watkins

on

Dylan Thomas

and other poets and poetry

SELECTED AND EDITED BY
GWEN WATKINS & JEFF TOWNS

WITH AN INTRODUCTION
BY DAVID WRIGHT

PARTHIAN

Parthian
The Old Surgery
Napier Street
Cardigan
SA43 1ED

www.parthianbooks.com

First published in 2013

ISBN 978 1 90984 405 6

Cover design by www.theundercard.co.uk
Typeset by typesetter.org.uk
Printed and bound by Gomer Press, Llandysul, Wales

The publisher acknowledges the financial support of the Welsh Books Council and the Rhys Davies Trust.

British Library Cataloguing in Publication Data

A cataloguing record for this book is available from the British Library.

This book is for Marley Watkins, my youngest grandchild, who will probably never read it, but whose skill and brilliance in football would have given untold pleasure to that other dedicated sportsman, his grandfather, Vernon Watkins.

G.M.W.

For Rosie Aslett, my eldest grandchild, who may, one day read this book, but for now wishes she could play football as well as Marley Watkins.

J.M.T.

Contents

VERNON WATKINS ON MODERN POETS

VERNON WATKINS ON ART AND ARTISTS

Foreword

By Rowan Williams

Vernon Watkins is very slowly finding his place again as a poet worthy of serious attention. His formal strictness as a writer, combined with the metaphysical complexity of some of his work has made readers over the last forty years or so unduly cautious and too easily discouraged. But the intensity of the best poems, their sheer disciplined intricacy as well as their metaphorical freshness, have begun to find a new public. In recent months, I was delighted that a reading of some of Watkins' poems to a student audience provoked enthusiasm and some astonishment: why hadn't they heard about him? Where could they read more?

But to develop acquaintance with and appreciation of Watkins, one has to give at least a little thought to what we expect poetry to be. Watkins was sparing in his theoretical observations on this subject, and would never have thought of himself as a critic. But he did, in letters, brief essays and occasional talks, set out something of a general or theoretical approach, and the pieces collected here allow us to see something of what he thought his business as a poet really was. Predictably, he warns against assuming that there is one and only one 'natural' voice for poetry overall or for any one poet in particular. It takes time and experience to discover a voice; no serious poet's idiom is just 'natural' speech, whatever a hasty reading of the preface to the *Lyrical Ballads* might suggest. Any poetic form is a thing discovered, laboured for, devised; not 'artificial' in the derogatory sense, but a work of artifice certainly. Finding how to be natural is, after all, a lifetime's ascetic work for human beings.

Such achieved naturalness comes in response to that 'second pressure' in poetry which denies us the use of the obvious things we are good at, moves us away from the fluency of a half-talent, requires us to invent a new language or register. This may be more or less obviously formal, more or less traditional, but what distinguishes it is that it has come out of a moment of abandoning the surface skills we began with, however spectacular. In these reflections, Watkins points again and again to the ways poets reinvent their own voices. We see how even Dylan Thomas (for many people an example of just that unreflective fluency Watkins challenges) is driven to move away from an idiom in both prose and poetry that depends unfairly on musicality and suggestive lyrical vagueness. And Yeats, of course, stands as the cardinal example of how to respond to the 'second pressure'.

Only a poetry schooled in this process of abandonment can escape the doom of being timebound. With sublimely unfashionable confidence, Watkins appeals to the 'eternal' that is coded in a poem; meaning not a poem's capacity to convey unspecific gusts of inspiration but its freedom to break into the conventional understanding of both its own era and others and enlarge the world of successive generations. Which is why, in perhaps his best known aphorism, Watkins identifies reputation as the real enemy of poetry.

These all too brief fragments and essays will prompt many to look again at Watkins's large and impressive body of work with new eyes, and, I hope, stimulate new questions and new kinds of attention for the poetic work of many others.

Rowan Williams

FOR VERNON WATKINS

This neat, slight man, a formal romantic
To whom the apparent was miracle,
Worked in a bank, romantically formal,
Framed constructs devised of rhetoric
As best to honour, best to penetrate
The oblique enigma of the visible.
He'd probe its miracle with that miraculous

Complex of passion, energy, music,
Correspondences of intuition,
Correspondences of the sensual, wit
Pushing its luck to reach beyond reason:
That artefact which makes exploration
Of actuality and of its nature,
Whose celebration becomes the poem.

Of a shed feather, scripture of water
Whose cursive, fast as it's written, fades
Where the sea tumbles, he, interpreter,
Will now no more walk on a cliff in Wales;
The dead man, humble and arrogant, leaves
His instruments carefully made and used:
Notations, images, and shapes of sound.

David Wright, October 1967

Introduction

Asked to write an introduction to this collection of Vernon Watkins' prose and critical essays, I was surprised to learn that he had written any. He had once told me that he did not write criticism. But he was wrong there, as I should have realized, for most of his letters to me were peppered with considered generalizations or specific criticisms of poetry and poems. And, having seen extracts of those he wrote to Michael Hamburger, some of which I propose to quote, I now think that Watkins' letters, should they ever be collected and published, would very probably prove a mine of critical insights and discernments.

The first time I met Vernon Watkins was in the late forties. As he had occupied an honoured pedestal in my private pantheon of contemporary poets ever since Sidney Keyes passed on to me a copy of 'Ballad of the Mari Lwyd' when we were undergraduates at Oxford together, I had sent him a copy of my first collection of verse – a dreadful production, which I would disown today if I could – and received a kind and perceptive, though not wholly uncritical, letter in reply. He mentioned that he was about to visit London; and when, most presumptuously as it seems to me now, I invited him to come to tea at my flat (I was then living above a bombed-out electric appliance shop in Great Ormond Street) he astonished me by agreeing. To this day I cannot understand why he should have bothered to accept an invitation from an unknown young man who had published a book of bad poems, was deaf, and for all he knew dumb as well. But he did come, bringing his wife Gwen and baby son, one dark winter afternoon; and from that moment there dated a friendship which, though hardly very close (I never visited Wales and he did not often come to London) was a permanent influence upon me and lasted till the day of his death in America. One unforgettable encounter was in the early '60s when my wife and I ran into him somewhere near Liberty's. He was accompanied by Gwen and his mother – a little old Welsh lady as fizzy as champagne. It was she who decided that we should then and there have tea together, led the conversation and commandeered the teapot. When the time came for second cups, finding us unimproved with a slopbowl, she solved the problem by offering the dregs as a libation to a potted plant on the windowsill, an action which caused the manager of the establishment to take a step in the direction of our table, only to be transfixed by her brilliant eye and confident 'Nothing better than tea! Nothing better!' as the old lady continued to feed cold slops to his fuchsia.

But, besides being one of a scarce breed – one of those who are poets first, last, and all the way through – Vernon Watkins was, I think, the most truly good human being I ever met. Two of his friends, Roy Campbell and Dylan Thomas, whom I came to know afterwards, were hardly paragons of conventional morality and behaviour; he knew all about that, but wouldn't and didn't make judgements or allow himself to think or believe ill of either. In fact it was Vernon Watkins' good opinion of him which went a long way to dissolve my initial prejudice against my countryman Roy Campbell, whom I then imagined – accepting the current hearsay myth – to be a fascist beast and bully, instead of the essentially humble, insecure, and magnanimous character he really was, and which Vernon, of course, had at once perceived.

Vernon Watkins was one of those rare poets – especially in our time – whose dedication to art was absolute and uncompromising. For more than forty years he worked as a cashier at the St Helen's Road branch of Lloyds bank in Swansea, refusing all promotion because he found the hours and duties interfered least with his desire to write poetry, while the salary enabled him to live without having to dissipate his energies or compromise his integrity by going in for some of the more paying forms of authorship: journalism, reviewing, writing for films or advertising; or by becoming a semi-academic and joining in the dance for creative chairs – though in Watkins' day that game had scarcely begun. As he remarked in answer to a questionnaire, he did not believe for a moment that a poet 'can, or should, earn enough money to live by writing only poetry. He would have to act as a window-dresser to his most secret property, and parade "that one talent which is death to hide", write in order to please, rather than to satisfy the thirst of the imagination.' All who knew him testify to that singleminded devotion to art and poetry. As his friend Philip Larkin attested in the memorial volume published by Faber after Watkins' death in 1967[1]: 'Despite his kindness, his whimsicality, his friendliness, there was something hard and brilliant about his attachment to poetry: he never hesitated. It was something there, tangible and palpable, commanding instant and unending allegiance... In Vernon's presence poetry seemed like a living stream, in which one only had to dip the vessel of one's devotion. He made it clear how one could, in fact, "live by poetry"; it was a vocation, at once difficult as sainthood and easy as breathing.'

Although Vernon Watkins had been writing verse since he was eight years old, it was not till he was thirty-five that he was persuaded to bring out his first volume of poems, 'The Ballad of the Mari Lwyd', which Faber and Faber published in 1941. He had little care for his own career as a poet; and one of his favourite aphorisms, which he would often reiterate with slight variations, was 'A poet need have only one enemy: his reputation.'

That was one of the many reasons why Watkins shied away from literary criticism. To Michael Hamburger he wrote in 1951 that he believed 'there can be no great criticism without love, and that the very nature and habit of most critics makes them incapable of an act of love. Their reputations are at stake, and they do not know what an excellent thing it would be to lose them.' He told Philip Larkin, among others, 'I would never review a living writer', and once wrote, more emphatically to Michael Hamburger: 'Any poet passing judgement on a living contemporary is damned'; which, as Hamburger remarked, 'was a strong word for Vernon to use, since he was as charitable as he was tolerant.' Again writing to

Hamburger, who had just published his book of criticism, 'Reason and Energy', Watkins expressed his doubts about the activity: 'My only criticism, so far of your book is that you pass relative judgment on poems. I suppose I represent the minority of one which believes that no critic does any service as to good and bad in anticipating the judgement of his readers. To present in terms of praise, which may be quantitative, is a different matter. Something inimitable has something secret about it. To compare productions in terms of "goodness", "merit", involves a comparison of the problems set in different works, and if that comparison is not exact and searching, the other comparison will be futile. Nearly all great critics do it, of course, but it still seems to me unjustified, and I always feel uneasy when it happens, as though I ought to clap, perhaps at the wrong time.'

Nonetheless – the book to which I am writing this introduction would otherwise not exist – Watkins did write a certain amount of criticism, sporadic and occasional as his essays seem to have been. It is fortunate that he did, for while Watkins cannot be described as a great critic, or even, perhaps, a critic at all according to contemporary standards – by which I mean nothing he wrote will conceivably help the average Eng. Lit. student to get a pass degree – what he had to say is valid and valuable as the credo of a poet and artist, and as a restatement for our time of truths and generalities that are ancient enough to seem new and profound enough for most people to gloss over. As is the way with poets, Watkins' criticism is an expression of his own poetic and philosophy rather than analysis and exegesis of the work of others. According to Hamburger, while Watkins was 'deeply distrustful of analytical, as distinct from intuitive, processes of any kind' he did approve of criticism based on 'voluntary enthusiasm for writers of one's own choice' because it 'must deepen one's understanding of them, just as translation in its laborious way brings to light much that was hidden or marginal in a poem. The critic I despise is that pontifical evaluator of contemporaries, the speculator in the poetic stock exchange, the soulless monster who has never heard of a widow's mite. I only despise him as a critic.'[2] In another letter Watkins goes on to say: 'Poetic criticism without quotation seems to me valueless. And general criticism such as I have seen in English periodicals – ("Why is it that the output of poetry in post-war Germany is, on the whole, disappointing?" etc.) seems equally valueless. The answer is obvious: "Sorry: the poetry factory has closed."' And yet again: 'Wisdom consists of crumbs, I think. I distrust the wide open spaces of competence.'

The articles collected in this volume show how well Watkins, in his critical essays, followed the guidelines laid down in his letters to Hamburger. His appraisals of Yeats, Wilfred Owen, and Dylan Thomas are not criticism as the word is usually understood. They are so full of quotation that they are like anthologies. His commentary on poems is generally appreciative: there is little of the elucidatory obfuscation with which your professional, that is to say academic, critic so dearly loves to defend the work of poets from lay enjoyment. There is none of that kind of microscopic exegesis which, so far from throwing light on a poem, is apt to stand between it and the light. Instead Watkins provides the occasional observation and generalization, illumined with the intuitive insight of a fellow-craftsman and artist, as when he says of Yeats' late poems that 'the last line is nearly always unpredictable; it is the moment, the moment of conscience. In all the late work the moment determines the poem. It is the swiftness of light rather than thought, and the leap from the good word to the unalterable word, which may be seen in Yeats' revisions, is like the sudden illumination of an object that had been kept in darkness. Yet these were aural revisions, never made for the eye; the light is musically controlled. The most delicate revisions, indeed, are sometimes made in words of different meaning but kindred sound, suggesting a statement which had first been imperfectly heard.' (Here I am reminded of what another poet, George Barker, once remarked to me in conversation, about the experience of writing a poem: 'It's like listening to a long-distance telephone call on a bad line.') Again, it is the craftsman and artist speaking when Watkins observes: 'In Yeats' technique the half-rhymes, subjugations of language and intimate darkening semitones are themselves a correction of expected rhyme, an intensely personal correction, and inseparable from the secret of his music.' Writing about Wilfred Owen, Watkins makes the perceptive observation: 'There is always, underlying poetry, the irony that poetry can achieve nothing actual.' One is reminded, of course, of Auden's famous line from 'In Memory of W. B. Yeats': 'For poetry makes nothing happen.' But Watkins goes on to say what Auden was perhaps incapable of seeing: 'it is this, more than anything else, that keeps a poet's work sincere.' The point is expanded in Watkins' later discussion of the extraordinary development of technique in Owen's late poems, when he remarks of Owen's 'Spring Offensive' that 'This poem shows again the paradox that Owen began to write great poetry as soon as he lost faith in poetry as an art.'

In the case of the poems of his friend Dylan Thomas, Watkins is of course able to speak from intimate personal knowledge. Thus he can clear up the surface obscurities of such poems as 'Once it was the Colour of Saying': It is a composite statement with several levels of interpretation. First of all, it is a very exact description of Dylan's work-room in the house at the top of Cwmdonkin Drive where he lived with his parents. I used to go there regularly at one time, especially on Saturday afternoons. His table was in front of the big bay-window facing West above the steep hill. Opposite were grass and trees, but I think he calls this "the uglier side of the hill" because it missed the view over Swansea Bay and the docks which were on the East side. Above this hill was Cwmdonkin Park, with its large reservoir. The "zoo of the willow-groves" has been cut down. The bandstand has gone. And in those days swans drifted on the water. Half-way down the hill, on the other side of the road, was a small playing-field, "cap-sized" as he describes it, only about a quarter of the size of a real one, where girls, dressed in black or white, came to practise hockey; capsized, too, on the sea of his imagination and the reservoir park of his childhood. "Where a school sat still" refers to the Deaf-and-Dumb school, also at the top of the hill. That is only one level of interpretation.'

But usefully informative as this kind of thing is – including the point that Thomas's famous poem, 'Do Not Go Gentle into that Good Night' which many people take to be an elegy for his father, was written eighteen months before the old man died in 1953 – a fact that I had myself forgotten, even though I can recall Thomas showing me the poem as early as 1952 at a poetry reading – far more revealing of Thomas as poet and performer is Watkins' vignette of him as a radio broadcaster: 'When he broadcast he found it necessary to take off his coat, for he used a great deal of invisible gesture. This was his true medium. In television he was magnificent, but physically uneasy, and he wore his coat.'

I have already quoted Watkins' remark, 'Wisdom consists of crumbs, I think.' While his longer disquisitions on individual poets obey his dictum that 'poetic criticism without quotation is valueless' the shorter essays tend to be aphoristic. In 1959, when Patrick Swift and I were editing the quarterly magazine 'X', I wrote to him to ask for a piece for a series called 'Poets on Poetry' that we were featuring (among the other poets who contributed were Hugh MacDiarmid, Jules Supervielle, Stevie Smith, Philip Jaccottet, Patrick Kavanagh, and Yves Bonnefoy) he replied that he did not write criticism; but in the end sent us a sheaf of gnomic maxims, obviously the refinement of much thought founded upon feeling and experience: hard diamonds of wisdom to meditate upon. Three of them have always seemed to me to be peculiarly apposite to Watkins' own work and outlook: 'The fountain, what is it? What is ancient, what is fresh.' 'Write for the dead, if you will not disappoint the living.' 'A true style cannot be learnt from contemporaries.'

These maxims were the basis of Watkins' thinking and poetic, and the ideas behind them are naturally enough repeated and elaborated in his other articles and pieces, as when he says in 'What is modern poetry?' 'The perception of a poet must be composite, as he is a witness for the living and the dead at the same time. If he observes the responsibilities, he will begin to see what is ancient in the contemporary scene and what is contemporary in the ancient; and his style will emerge from that collision, from that twofold perception,' or again, in 'Problems of Communication': 'A poet does not only address a living audience; equally he addresses the dead and the unborn.' It is in fact quite astonishing how compactly Watkins expresses what he has to say, how epigrammatically he compresses his thought. In a single short essay, 'Theory and Act' one finds the following: 'The strictest French poetry is Villon's and it is at once the sparest and most exuberant. Every avenue of expression is open to him because he has chosen a narrow road. Intensity of belief, far from restricting a poet, gives him range. A metaphysical poet, whether he be Donne or Blake or Yeats, cannot write without being involved in belief, and his belief is tested by every contact with life, and renewed every day. Without a compass, there is no voyage. The needle trembles, but it returns to the same point. Apophthegms are scattered throughout the essays: 'A city has no right to be remembered except for what a materialist would call its wasteful productions' and 'It is the relationship of the artist to himself that matters to the public. He is, as it were, caught up in a conversation which is only made clear by the work he produces.' And finally, his credo, not easily arrived at, nor cursorily offered: 'I am convinced that the foundation of art is joy.'

October 1982
David Wright

[1] Vernon Watkins 1906-1967 Leslie Norris, 1970

[2] Vernon Watkins to Michael Hamburger, 20.03.1952

Aphorisms

X. A Quarterly Review Poets on Poetry I
Vernon Watkins

Natural speech may be excellent, but who will remember it unless it is allied to something artificial, to a particular order of music?

Criticism projects its high tone, its flattering responses, but of what man-made echo does the mind not weary, as it turns endlessly round the Earth?

Ambition is wholly imitative and wholly competitive until it has died.

Unredeemed ambition is the desire to survive the present. Its direction is despair.

Redeemed ambition is the willingness to die rather than accept a survival alien to present truth. Its direction is compassion.

Religious poetry is sealed like the eyes of Lazarus by a refusal to be raised except by the true God.

The fountain, what is it? What is ancient, what is fresh. Defects of the imagination are always reflected in style.

Vagueness is an enemy of holiness; the soul of harmony continually thirsts for definition.

The epic depends on exactness of detail: the larger the theme, the more minute its organization.

The syllable is the strictest instructor. For the lyric poet what better critic than silence?

A poet need have only one enemy: his reputation.

Write for the dead, if you will not disappoint the living.

The stammerer may arrive at the truth the fluent speaker missed.

A true style cannot be learnt from contemporaries.

A fragmentary statement of truth is better than a polished falsification, for how could that live, even for a moment, beside what is eternally fresh?

What is revision except, in the interests of unity, to eliminate the evidence of words?
Suffering is a great teacher: we know nothing until we know that.

Lyric poetry at its best is the physical body of what the imagination recognizes as truth.

The point of balance in a poem is unpredictable. Whatever weight a poet brings to it, beyond a certain point the poem writes itself.

Composition is spontaneous, but true spontaneity in poetry is nearly always a delayed thing. It is the check, the correction, the transfigured statement, that makes the poem unforgettable.

A poet, overhearing a conversation out of time, must be his time's interpreter; but how can the Muse know this, whose eyes are fixed on what is eternally fresh and continually beginning?

Critics, even unimportant ones, are bound to demonstrate their vitality, like sandhoppers.

The true critic, the true discoverer, stays in the same place.

The true poem renews itself at its close.

Art is miraculous. There is no destructive or restrictive theory of art which cannot be contradicted by a work of genius.

Vernon Watkins on Dylan Thomas

A Note on Dylan Thomas

It is difficult to explain to anyone who did not know Dylan Thomas why any study of him must remain totally inadequate. It is equally difficult to explain why those who knew him find themselves deeply handicapped in writing about him. The quality he prized most was seriousness, and he was a born clown; but was there any other poet of recent times who could create so quickly an intimacy of judgement, an apprehension of what was valid, in life and in art? That is perhaps one of the reasons why strangers who met him only once for a long conversation felt, after his death, that they had known him all their lives. The entertainer and the intellectual alike were slightly ashamed after meeting him as he could beat them both at their own game, but if they were humble they quickly recognized that he was humble too. The prig was his bête noire, the pedant a black and white crossword figure whom he didn't despise.

The variety of life and its abundance sang in his veins.

He was born to praise it, and he did so most completely when war distorted it into every manifestation of horror. When the war ended, his own war continued. He was, on the one hand, enriched by the heroic comedy of people's lives, for he loved people, and, on the other, fascinated by artificial pattern, for the problems of form he had to solve in his last poems were subtler and more intricate than any he had set himself before. He found freedom in the late broadcast scripts, but pattern obsessed him. In this late work the prose, with all its humorous invention, was made by his social life, the poetry by his isolation in spite of that, the isolation of the entertainer who has taken off his mask.

A writer's mask can be fatal to him, and it is certain that the image demanded of Dylan Thomas was accelerated by his popularity. His infectious humour deceived everyone but himself. His method was not to retreat from the mask, but to advance beyond it, and in that exaggeration remain completely himself. He agreed readily with his detractors, and did not at all mind being misunderstood. Then, in the private dark, his exuberance was subjected to the strictest control. The public figure and the lyric poet whose work began and ended in the Garden of Eden came to terms, terms which no critic or friend has the complete equipment to analyse.

Notes on Dylan Thomas

When I met Dylan Thomas he was twenty and already beginning to be well known. He had published his first book, *18 Poems*, and this had created a sensation. These poems were quite unlike anything else in contemporary literature, here or abroad. They were intricate poems, packed with sexual imagery. They were musical and symmetrical. They were explorations of the universe always related back to the poet's own body, to his forbears, to time and dissolution, to birth and its mystery. The book was remarkable for all these things, but it was most remarkable of all for a new idiom, a new type of poetic statement, intensely personal to the poet, which announced itself on every page.

I see the summer children in their mothers
Split up the brawned womb's weathers,
Divide the night and day with fairy thumbs;
There in the deep with quartered shades
Of sun and moon they paint their dams
As sunlight paints the shelling of their heads.

***

The force that through the green fuse drives the flower
Drives my green age...

***

I sit and watch the worm beneath my nail
Wearing the quick away.

***

When, like a running grave, time tracks you down,...
Comes, like a scissors stalking, tailor age...

***

Light breaks where no sun shines;
Where no sea runs, the waters of the heart
Push in their tides;
And, broken ghosts with glow-worms in their heads,
The things of light
File through the flesh where no flesh decks the bones.

A candle in the thighs
Warms youth and seed and burns the seeds of age...

These examples reveal the idiom well enough, and the lines are all unmistakably his own. They do not appear to be derivative from any English poet of a past generation; certainly they owed nothing to his contemporary poets. Yet it would be difficult to find, except in Rimbaud, a poet under twenty with so sure a power to contract and define. Because the subject of these poems is mystery, their effect is rarely entirely lucid. The poet is projecting the world of his imagination upon the observed world in a density of vision tested, again and again, by the beat of the blood. They are haunted by Freudian symbols, and they use the materials of the natural world to express joy or wonder, horror or dissatisfaction, always in physical terms, terms of adolescence, manhood, organic growth and decay.

I remember turning over the pages of this book in the bookshop in Swansea where I first found it. I would do this guiltily as I did not intend to buy it. I was completely absorbed in writing poetry myself, so the last thing I wanted in the house was a book by another living poet of my own generation. I looked to Yeats as the great living master of poetry, and I did not really want a contemporary, nor did I expect to find one.

It was with these impressions in my mind, and with the book finally bought against my will and installed, rather uncomfortably, in my room, that I met Dylan Thomas for the first time. He had just returned from London. I had left a message at his home in Cwmdonkin Drive for him to ring me up when he returned. He rang up and came out on a Saturday afternoon. I remember that first meeting very clearly. He was slight, shorter than I had expected, shy and eager in manner, deep-voiced, restless, humorous, with large, wondering, yet acutely intelligent eyes, gold curls, and under these the face of a cherub. We immediately went for a walk on the cliffs. We had not gone far when I realized that this cherub took nothing, either in thought or words, for granted, but rather challenged everything with the instinct of a stubborn nature guarding its own freshly discovered truth.

We soon became very close friends, and my first impression of that rooted obstinacy, which was really a rooted innocence, was reinforced whenever we met. We met often, either at his house or mine, and usually we spent half the evening reading poems to each other. At our first meeting, after that walk, I read him some of my poems. On the first evening I spent with him in Cwmdonkin Drive he began to read his own. He unfolded a large file, marked in block capitals 'POMES'. The first poem he read to me was 'Ears in the Turrets Hear...' and he followed this with others which he intended to print in his second book, 'Twenty-Five Poems'. Last of all he read the sonnet sequence, of which he had then written seven, beginning 'Altar-wise by Owl-light in the Half-way House'. The last three sonnets, of the Crucifixion, Egyptian burial, and the Resurrection, were written during the next few weeks, and these formed the ten which were printed at the end of 'Twenty-five Poems'.

Every week we met, at least once, for the evening either in Swansea or Pennard. And every Wednesday we also met for coffee or lunch at the Kardomah, with Fred Janes, Tom Warner, the composer, Charlie Fisher, who was on the *South Wales Evening Post*, John Prichard, poet and novelist, and others. Daniel Jones would certainly have been there, but he was studying music at this time in Italy and Austria. I had not met him then, but he was an almost legendary figure in the conversation. Dylan had so many stories about him that I felt I knew him personally. Once, I was challenged to describe him, which I did, in fairly exact detail, and the detail turned out to be right. Either Dylan had told me more than I remembered or else he supplied me, at that moment, with a telepathic photograph.

Besides poetry, Dylan read me stories. He had finished 'The Orchards', which afterwards was to be collected with other early stories in the prose section of 'The Map of Love'. It was in this story that the name Llareggub first appeared, 'the Black Book of Llareggub'. It was a trick name, to be read in reverse; Dylan alone could have thought of so Welsh an invention, but it was also an example of the word-play he had learnt from Joyce, whom he admired more than any other prose writer. 'Llareggub' became, much later, the provisional title of 'Under Milk Wood', and was printed as such in the first half of the version published in 'Botteghe Oscure' in 1952.

Dylan showed me the manuscript of 'The Orchards'. The whole story was written in minute handwriting on the inside cover of a cardboard box. He told me that it helped him to see the whole story in one place as he wrote it, and pages were less good for this than box-covers.

Some of the stories showed an almost surrealist imagination, but this did not appear in the poems, and as an influence on his work it did not last long. He did, though, enjoy the Surrealist Exhibition in 1938, where a learned lecture was given in a packed room accompanied by an electric bell which made every word inaudible. Everyone had been asked to do something, he said. He himself had boiled some string and handed it round to people in cups.

Another story Dylan read me at this time was 'The Lemons' which *Life and Letters* printed afterwards. In this he explored almost scientifically the link between the interior and exterior worlds, for the two were still mysteriously separated in his imagination, and in his poetry and his prose he was still much more conscious of the first than of the second. But the best story of this period was one which he read to me before he had finished it. It was to be called 'A View of the Sea', and was to be dedicated to his friend Tom Warner who had written a piece of music with that title. Dylan was always ready to accept suggestions, and he would make small changes if the alteration appealed to his imagination more strongly, but only after he had tested it many times on his tongue. One of these made it necessary to change the title, which now became 'A Prospect of the Sea'.

Dylan was now preparing his second book of poems, 'Twenty-five Poems', and they were almost finished. He liked these poems, for the most part, much better than the poems of the first book. He read me the first long poem, 'I, In My Intricate Image...', a poem in three parts which has seventy-two variations in line-endings on the letter 'L', twenty-four in each part. These variations were so subtly used that they did not at all obtrude, and the scheme, like that of the 'Prologue' to the 'Collected Poems', was only unfolded after a reading of the poem to the retrospective observation. Dylan said that he did not think it a successful poem, but that he liked it as well as anything he had done up to that time. The statement was modest, but Dylan was always modest about his poems, though he was really very sure of them. Other poems of the book which he was just finishing were 'Then was my

Neophyte' and 'To-day This Insect and the World I Breathe', both of which came out in the Autumn, 1936 number of the magazine 'Purpose'. Edith Sitwell had in *The London Mercury* written about the beautiful poem 'A Grief Ago', and her praise was the first really emphatic eulogy of Dylan's poetry to reach a wide public. Besides confessing the excitement and overwhelming effect the poem had produced when she read it, she gave an analysis of its parts, investigating its mysterious force through sound-values, and attempting to sift its compound meanings. Dylan appreciated her analysis and praise, but he did not really agree with her siftings of meaning. He always spoke of her with affection, and when there was a series of letters in the Sunday papers attacking his poetic method it was she who answered them brilliantly. Dylan himself never wrote, but, after one particularly rude letter from a member of the Adelphi Club, he asked me whether the paper would print a reply asking the member to meet him on the steps of the Athenaeum Club so that he could hit him.

I tried to persuade Dylan to leave two of the poems out of 'Twenty-Five Poems', the poems beginning 'Now, say nay...' and 'How Soon the Servant Sun'. Their obscurity really amounted to meaninglessness, at least for me, which was not true of any of the other poems. All of them seemed packed with meaning. Of one of these two poems Dylan remarked that so far as he knew it had no meaning at all. He was, however, firm about including them. When I said that reviewers would be likely to pick on these rather than the fine poems in the book he smiled and said, 'Give them a bone'.

The one poem which Dylan hesitated about including

was one which is very well known. When I called at Cwmdonkin Drive he had almost decided to leave out 'And Death Shall Have No Dominion'. Certainly he said he would leave it out unless he altered it. I said how much I liked it, and admired its rhythm, and, with a few very small changes, he became quite satisfied with it. 'Dead men naked' had originally been 'gentlemen naked' in the second line; and 'Heads of the gentlemen hammer through daisies' was also altered to 'Heads of the characters'.

The only other revisions which I remember Dylan making in these poems were in the 'neophyte' poem, where I persuaded him to alter a line about his undeveloped self, and in the poem 'Should Lanterns Shine' where he cut the last two lines of the poem as it had been printed in Geoffrey Grigson's review, 'New Verse'. I suggested that those two lines, about the moon shining on the lawn and the lawn lying beneath the moon, which seemed to echo Eliot and, indirectly, Laforgue, should be scrapped; and he decided to end the poem without them. The two previous lines, with their hidden nuances, made a fine autobiographical ending:

> The ball I threw while playing in the park
> Has not yet reached the ground.

From this time forward, Dylan sent me his poems more or less as he finished them. I typed them for him, and we exchanged many letters about them. I typed all the poems for his next book, 'The Map of Love', containing poems and stories, which was published by Dent in 1939. The excitement I felt when I opened these poems was always great, and they usually came one at a time. He was a slow and patient craftsman, and he had become slower since the early poems. The second poem of the book, written for his wife, certainly took six months of more or less continuous writing. His method of composition was itself painfully slow. He used separate work-sheets for individual lines, sometimes a page or two being devoted to a single line, while the poem was gradually built up, phrase by phrase. He usually had beforehand an exact conception of the poem's length, and he would decide in advance to allot so many lines to a particular part of its development. The force of utterance has sometimes concealed the symmetry which was so strong an element in all his work. Yet he recognized that, in spite of all his care and power of construction, it was for the sake of divine accidents that a poem existed at all. Because of this, in spite of our entirely different methods, there was always the deepest affinity between us. He began with a core of meaning, with a piece of clay which he moulded in his hands. The music of the poem came later. In the handling of texture he had wit and great mastery, and music was really a later stage in the action of the poem. He certainly did not let it govern what he wanted to say. My own verse composition began with music and arrived, most laboriously, at texture. Dylan helped me a great deal. His first demand of a poem was that it should be fresh and alive. I had written at least five hundred poems before we met, but that was because I was nearly thirty and had been writing poetry ever since I was a small boy. He liked 'After Sunset' and 'Thames Forest', both poems which were still unfinished after two or three years' work when I met him; but there was much that he did not like, much that showed a love of poetry rather than an ability to write it. His fresh eye taught me a lot, and helped me to remove many archaisms.

There was, then, great friendship and no rivalry between us. I recognized at once that he was doing what I could not do, and I had faith in his genius. I realised that he was a true poet of a different kind. Our great bond was that we were both religious poets, but his sense of rhythm, his vocabulary, his idiom, were all different from mine. I tested my work by a discipline which he had now made familiar, and I liked to think of it as improving under that discipline. It was a fundamental belief of mine that a poet could not learn how to write from his contemporaries, but only from himself and from ancient poets. Dylan did, however, often show me where I went wrong. Years later, when I read poems at Oxford, I was asked how I reconciled my conviction about learning only from ancient poets to my admission that Dylan had influenced my attitude to writing deeply. I answered: "Dylan IS an ancient poet, but he happens to be alive."

Dylan shared my admiration for Yeats whom he considered easily the greatest living poet. After Yeats, he thought that Eliot had the best ear; but his favourite poet of the century, bad or good, was Hardy. When he asked me what I chiefly wanted to write about I said, 'Grief, and time'. But he understood that I could never write a poem dominated by time, as Hardy could. This, in fact, was also true of Dylan, though some critics have mistakenly thought to find such poems in his work. It illustrates our affinity on a deeper level; his poems spoke to me with the voice of metaphysical truth, and his choice of theme was very close to mine. We had nothing in common with the sociological, reforming poets of the time. Among these he certainly liked W. H. Auden best, though he usually disliked his themes. I remember particularly one morning when we met in the Kardomah. The talk turned to modern poets and he announced that the Editor of 'New Verse' had asked him for a tribute to Auden for an Auden double-number of the magazine. He sent a short tribute, full of enthusiastic praise, but he added a Postscript: 'Congratulations on Auden's seventieth birthday.'

It was just at this time, or a little before this, that Keidrych Rhys founded his magazine 'Wales'. Dylan took two poems of mine for the first number, and he contributed a short prose piece, 'Prologue to an Adventure' which, on account of indiscreet words, provoked over a hundred letters of protest to the 'Western Mail'. To later numbers he sent several of the fine poems which were afterwards printed in 'The Map of Love'. Other poems destined for the same book appeared in 'Life and letters'. 'Wales', though a small paper, had quite a success for a short time and sold well in America. A good deal of the success of the early numbers was, I think, due to Dylan's contributions.

It was now proposed by Dent's, his publishers, that Dylan should write a book about Wales, and they commissioned him to travel around the country for that purpose. He got as far as London, and stayed there. He explained later that he couldn't write about Wales in Wales. Nor could he write that kind of book at all. Instead, he was beginning to write stories about human beings living and behaving exactly as they used to live and behave when he was a child. He had abruptly abandoned the highly charged, intensely symbolic style of his early stories, and all his work moved now in the direction of the living voice. He wrote these stories quickly, as his imagination, insofar as people were concerned, was a well-spring of humorous invention which could only be compared with Dickens. They were exact and extremely witty accounts of his boyhood and youth in and around Swansea, his home town. Meanwhile a selection of the early stories, which contained so much less of himself, so much more that was artificial, appeared in 1939 in the prose section of 'The Map of Love', and the best of them, 'A Prospect of the Sea', for some reason known only to the publishers, had been omitted.

'The Map of Love' was, however, a fine book, and certainly the best and the deepest that he had published. Herbert Read saluted the poems of this volume by saying that they contained 'the most absolute poetry that had been written in our time'.

Dylan sent me all these poems, as I have said. If he was uncertain of a particular passage or word in a poem he used to mention this in the letter accompanying it. Sometimes, as in the case of the first poem of the book, he was uncertain of the poem's length. The poem originated probably in a dream of his about a blind horse which began to sing. A man had said, 'He sings better now.'

The poem begins:

'Because the pleasure-bird whistles after the hot wires,
Shall the blind horse sing sweeter?
Convenient bird and beast lie lodged to suffer
The supper and knives of a mood.'

And the comment in the accompanying letter was this: '... Here's a new poem. Tell me: is it too short? Do I end before the point? Does it need more room to work to a meaning, any expansion? I intended it as a longer and more ambitious thing, but stopped it suddenly thinking it was complete.' He did not add to it at all, or alter it.

When I received the famous poem in memory of Ann Jones it was only fifteen lines long, the first fifteen lines. {It} was the first poem Dylan had written about his relationship to one individual and to her whole life. It was his first statement of an intensely religious and yet intensely personal belief, the love of God reconciling apparently irreconcilable human attitudes. It was also the first poem, and the only poem before those in 'Deaths and Entrances' to which he gave a title. I had suggested titles to him from our first meeting, but he did not see why a poet should use them any more than a composer did for his music.

He had used only numbers and first lines.

The little poem following 'In Memory of Ann Jones', which begins:

Once it was the colour of saying
Soaked my table the uglier side of a hill
With a capsized field where a school sat still
And a black and white patch of girls grew playing:

is about the room in the house in Cwmdonkin Drive where he wrote many poems. Its wide windows looked across the road to a sloping field where girls used to play hockey. The school was the deaf-and-dumb school. The poem goes on:

The gentle seaslides of saying I must undo
That all the charmingly drowned arise to cockcrow
  and kill.
When I whistled with mitching boys through a
  reservoir park
Where at night we stoned the cold and cuckoo
Lovers in the dirt of their leafy beds,
The shade of their trees was a word of many shades
And a lamp of lightning for the poor in the dark;
Now my saying shall be their undoing,
And every stone I wind off like a reel.

This little poem, which to me is a poem on two levels and a marvel of condensation, represents a repudiation of style as decisive as that of Yeats, when he wrote his own little poem 'A Coat':

I made my song a coat
Covered with embroideries
Out of old mythologies
From heel to throat;
But the fools caught it,
Wore it in the world's eyes
As though they'd wrought it.
Song, let them take it
For there's more enterprise
In walking naked.

The poems in 'The Map of Love' differ fundamentally from the earlier poems. The first poems were exuberant exercises of an imagination discovering its richness and the richness of the world; they created their own astonishment with daring innovations which yet showed an ancient handling of language and a biblical influence; but these poems unmask the innovator as a religious poet, and each part of them is controlled by the religious sense. Their hesitation, their stillness, is a source of intuitive strength.

The art of composition is a most mysterious thing. Certainly the closest approximation to truth is found in the Greek conception of the Muse. It would be impossible to write great poetry with confidence alone. At least nine-tenths of the work is done by listening. Dylan knew this, but he did not wait particularly for the Muse to catch him. He was absorbed in life and in people. He did not know where his next poem would come from, and he did not care. He only cared at all when he had begun to write it. He read all kinds of books, and at this time every thriller he could find, and he loved films, however bad. A really bad film gave him an acute sensation which he could not resist.

In whatever place or circumstance, Dylan had a jackdaw's eye for what he wanted; and when he had found it, he treasured it zealously and kept it for use later on. I remember him coming to my house one day in a state of excitement. He had been given his next poem by a particularly dull thriller in which his eye had suddenly fallen on the sentence: 'The shadow is dark directly under the candle'. The poem he projected from this statement is the poem about churches, the fifth poem in 'The Map of Love', the poem beginning:

It is the sinners' dust-tongued bell claps me to churches
When, with his torch and hourglass, like a sulphur
priest,
His beast heel cleft in a sandal,
Time marks a black aisle kindle from the brand of ashes,
Grief with dishevelled hands tear out the altar ghost
And a firewind kill the candle.

Over the choir minute I hear the hour chant:
Time's coral saint and the salt grief drown a foul
sepulchre
And a whirlpool drives the prayerwheel;
Moonfall and sailing emperor, pale as their tide-print,
Hear by death's accident the clocked and dashed-down
spire
Strike the sea hour through bellmetal.

There is loud and dark directly under the dumb flame...

That is one illustration of the unpredictable source. There are many instances of his treasuring single elements through poems which he finally discarded and using them later in poems where they found their inevitable place. His instinct had told him that they were necessary to his work before the new poem made a place for them. The two lines about wolves in the next to last verse of the long second poem of 'The Map of Love' had once formed part of a separate composition, and the very last words of the last poem

For as long as forever is

had been the opening of a poem the first verse of which he had read to me. The poem had been scrapped and two years had gone when this postcard arrived:

BIRTHDAY POEM

Twenty-four years remind the tears of my eyes.
(Bury the dead for fear that they walk to the grave in
labour.)
In the groin of the natural doorway I crouched like a
tailor
Sewing a shroud for a journey
By the light of the meat-eating sun.
Dressed to die, the sensual strut begun,
With my red veins full of money,
In the final direction of the elementary town
I advance for as long as forever is.

Beneath the poem was this note:

'This very short poem is for my birthday just arriving. I know you'll hate the use of the "Forever" line, but there it is. I scrapped the poem beginning with that line long ago, and at last – I think – I've found the inevitable place for it: it was a time finding that place. I'm pleased, terribly, with this – so far. Do tell me, and type please. In the first version I had "like a stuffed tailor". I think stuffed is wrong, don't you? Try to read the end of the poem as though you didn't know the lines. I do feel they're right. In the old "Forever" poem they were completely out of place – and the rest of the poem wouldn't stand without them. So bang went the whole poem, obviously, and here at last is what it should be.'

It was now the Autumn of 1938. Before this great, little poem, Dylan had worked intensively for many months on the long poem about burial, finished in April, beginning;

> How shall my animal
> Whose wizard shape I trace in the cavernous skull,
> Vessel of abscesses and exultation's shell,
> Endure burial under the spelling wall,
> The invoked, shrouding veil at the cap of the face,
> Who should be furious,
> Drunk as a vineyard snail, flailed like an octopus,
> Roaring, crawling, quarrel
> With the outside weathers,
> The natural circle of the discovered skies
> Draw down to its weird eyes?

We exchanged letters about this poem which I admired so much, letters concerned only with two or three particular words, but in nearly every letter I had from Dylan there was an intuitive statement about poetry or life which only he could make. He was now working on the two long poems at the end of 'The Map of Love'. His wife was expecting her first child in January, and the two poems are about birth. When he was halfway through the longer poem he quoted the first stanza to me from memory. There are three stanzas. The first is full of exaltation and mystery. The second brings heaven down to earth; and the third sets against the imminence of lunacy and war the exaltation of birth itself. The reality of birth is presented with great violence, and the born child is declared holy and full of joy against all the unholy and unjoyful arguments against that miracle. He is presented in the last stanza as stronger than all the opposing forces.

This poem was finished in December, 1938, just a month before Llewelyn was born, a couple of days after the death of Yeats.

As soon as he had finished it he set to work upon the second poem about birth which is in dialogue form, the dialogue being spoken first by the unborn child and then by the mother. He sent me the poem early in March. The poem moved me very much. I do not remember what I said about it, but I have his letter answering mine in which he says:

'I agreed with every word you wrote about my poem. The second person speaks better than the first, and the last line is false. I haven't been able to alter the first part, and will have to leave it unsuccessful. The last line is now "And the endless beginning of prodigies suffers open". I worked on from your suggestion.

'I'd like to go over the final proofs of all the poems with you, but that won't be for a few weeks... Did I tell you the book, which will be priced at 7/6 and have a John portrait, includes 7 short stories as well. All unviolent ones. Church refuses to pass the best "P. of the Sea", because of its "unwarrantable moments of sensuality"– the fish.'

'The Map of Love' was ready, and Dylan had already written several of the Swansea stories for his next book, 'Portrait of the Artist as a Young Dog.'

These stories with the background of childhood came to him quickly. Most were written at Laugharne where I stayed with him often, and he would read them aloud. By the end of 1939 they were finished.

The stories released a stream of humorous invention

which Dylan had kept out of his poetry but which was very much a part of himself. He was an astonishing mimic, and when he read a book aloud to me he would give a different voice to each character. He read several of Caradoc Evans's books in that way. To me the reading was a revelation as I hardly read prose at all, and when I did I found it difficult to dramatize what I was reading. This defect amounted to an abnormality. We were having tea once with his parents in Bishopston when his father turned to me and said, 'Dylan is so narrow in his reading. There are so many books that he won't read.' 'Narrow!' Dylan said. '*Me* narrow? Why, *he* stops as soon as the words go on to the edge of the page.'

My only objection to the 'Portrait of the Artist' stories was the title. I thought the book ought to be titled 'One Warm Saturday' after the last story. But Dylan was firm. Besides, his publishers had said that it was a good selling title. I could not see how the stories, as reproductions of his boyhood, could be improved; but he used to say that although he was very glad he had written them they could not compare to Joyce's 'Dubliners'. Perhaps not. But I do not believe for a moment that Joyce could have written 'The Peaches', 'The Fight', or 'Extraordinary Little Cough'.

So 'Portrait of the Artist as a Young Dog' was given to Dent's in place of the book about Wales which they had asked for. After the effort of the poems of 'The Map of Love' the writing of the stories had been for Dylan a relaxation. He now turned to poems again. He believed that there was no assured place for a poet, that in each new poem he must start from scratch. His development now was in the direction of a barer lyricism. The tricks and puns and word-inversions he had inherited from Joyce now played a smaller part in his composition. He was concerned solely with the presentation of all the holy parts of a single vision.

It was, I think, in 1940 that we met at the Empire Theatre in Swansea for a performance of Mozart's 'Marriage of Figaro'. Just before the opera began he told me that he had begun a new poem with the words:

On almost the incendiary eve
Of several near deaths...

It was to be called 'Deaths and Entrances' and this was to be the title of his next book 'because', he said, 'it is all I ever write about or have written about.' He now used titles for his poems. The little poem 'Paper and Sticks' he had read to me long before, and two others had been written which were to be collected in this book. One, 'On the Marriage of a Virgin', had first of all only one stanza, the first. That is how I received it; the second stanza was added later. And 'Love in the Asylum' had been written quickly as soon as the long, six-month poem for Caitlin, the second poem in 'The Map of Love,' had been finished.

Yet the poems of 'Deaths and Entrances', which are, with the very last, his greatest poems, were nearly all of slow evolution. One of the most beautiful, the poem for his birthday beginning 'It was my thirtieth year to Heaven', was first quoted to me as 'It was my twenty-seventh year to Heaven'. Even the quickly written poem 'Love in the Asylum' which opens:

A stranger has come
To share my room in the house not right in the head,
was first tried out in another form, with a comic beginning:
'They have put another lunatic into my cell'.

The short poem 'On a Wedding Anniversary' is an example of a drastic rewriting after its first printed form, and Dylan sent me an early version of 'Unluckily for a Death' which is quite different from that finally printed in the book. The changes always represented a movement away from irony in the direction of religious truth. One has only to compare the last stanza of 'Unluckily for a Death' as it was sent to me first with its final revision. Here is the unpublished stanza:

Love, my fate got luckily,
May teach me now with no telling
That every drop of water is both kind and cruel,
With articulate eyes
Tell me the money-coloured sun sees poorly,
Teach that the child who sucks on innocence
Is spinning fast and loose on a fiery wheel,
All that we do, cruelly, kindly,
Will kiss in a huddle:
In the teeth of that black-and-white wedding
I chuck my armed happiness.
Though the puffed phoenix stir in the rocks
And lucklessly fair or sycorax the widow wait,
We abide with our pride, the unalterable light,
On this turning lump of mistakes.

And here is the published version:

Love, my fate got luckily,
Teaches with no telling
That the phoenix' bid for heaven and the desire after
Death in the carved nunnery
Both shall fail if I bow not to your blessing
Nor walk in the cool of your mortal garden
With immortality at my side like Christ the sky.
This I know from the native
Tongue of your translating eyes. The young stars told me,
Hurling into beginning like Christ the child.
Lucklessly she must lie patient
And the vaulting bird be still. O my true love, hold me.
In your every inch and glance is the globe of genesis
spun,
And the living earth your sons.

The advent of war filled Dylan with such horror and such a sense of world lunacy that his only thought was to continue in his poetry the praise of everything that war crushed and rejected. He was now working on a new poem, a poem entirely in assonance, and he wrote to me saying that this poem moved him more than anything he had done for a long time. He would not send it yet as it was not finished; but later he did. Here are the first two verses:

There was a saviour
Rarer than radium,
Commoner than water, crueller than truth:
Children kept from the sun
Assembled at his tongue
To hear the golden note turn in a groove,

Prisoners of wishes locked their eyes
In the jails and studies of his keyless smiles.

The voice of children says
From a lost wilderness
There was calm to be done in his safe unrest,
When hindering man hurt
Man, animal, or bird
We hid our fears in that murdering breath,
Silence, silence to do, when earth grew loud,
In lairs and asylums of the tremendous shout.

This was really the first of the entirely assonantal poems. Dylan had from the first preferred the method of mixing rhymes and half-rhymes, but his test for a rhyme was that you should not expect it. He certainly did not like writing in unrhymed form, but he also disliked, as he once said, having his rhymes labelled for him. He wanted to preserve a strictness of choice in language with which direct rhyme sometimes interfered. So he usually resorted to dissonance or assonance and built his stanzas on a fabric of exact language in which the line-endings were musically and mathematically balanced, but did not reproduce the sound that had gone before. The device is so successful in his very finest poems, like 'It was my Thirtieth Year to Heaven' and 'Fern Hill', that it is not too much to say that Dylan created with these poems a new emotional form, and a new stanza form for English poetry, in which they are masterpieces.

I saw Dylan a great deal when he was writing the 'Ballad of the Long-Legged Bait', and I saw this poem grow from its first fifteen lines through all the stages of its composition. He wrote the four-lined verses in pairs. The poem is full of visual imagery. It was so much a visual poem that he made a coloured picture for it which he pinned on the wall of his room, a picture of a woman lying at the bottom of the sea. She was a new Loreley revealing the pitfalls of destruction awaiting those who attempted to put off the flesh.

The Ballad had been written in 1940/41, mainly at Bishopston, but now he was back in Laugharne, and on the very day that war was declared a friend motored me down to see him. There were a lot of soldiers in the pub there, and some deserters were drinking with the escorts who had come to collect them and who had practically decided to desert, too. The room in the pub on that evening was one of the most confused rooms I have ever seen. Outside it was the hill, Laugharne Castle, and the estuary, the landscape that he would write about in 'Over Sir John's Hill' and the last poems. He loved it, and he hated everything to do with the war; and he knew that very soon he would have to decide whether to register as a conscientious objector or for military service.

Dylan did, in fact, make this decision in a rather unexpected way. He felt that it would be best and most logical to be a conscientious objector, but he had to attend a tribunal for conscientious objectors in Wales as a witness. As each objector came forward he was asked on what grounds he objected to military service, and in each case a mean little voice answered, ''ligious'. Each was then asked what he was prepared to do, and each answered, in an even meaner little voice, 'Nothing'. When Dylan left this court he felt that one door was closed to him, and later, when his own turn came, he confessed to me that he had signed for the army, but as a never-fighter. 'Talk about the lads of the land,' he said, describing his call-up. 'most of them were twisted with rheumatism and none looked under fifty. The man next to me said he would join the Navy as he wanted to fly. He was classified D4, and I was C3.'

Dylan was, for the time being, exempted from military service, and my turn, as I was eight years older, had not come. I was in the Home Guard. Someone suggested that I should join the Army Field Security Service and learn to ride a motor-bike, but I decided that the war would end before I managed this. Dylan's advice to me was: 'Be a censor; pry and erase.' He was now living in a big house near Chippenham, owned by John Davenport, where a lot of artists stayed, along with writers, painters and musicians. He wrote to me from there:

'I'm in debt, and need my job quickly. Perhaps we're both marked. You translate Hölderlin and swear in German to the Home Guards; I have no visible means of support, and have been known to call the war bloody and silly. I hope there's a special censor for our letters: a man who keeps a miserable family on the strength of attempting to decode our innocent messages.'

We continued to send poems to each other, and to say exactly what we thought about them. Dylan's criticism was always acute, and it was always made from the point of view of composition, just as his reading aloud always stemmed from the creation of the poem, rather than its utility. Just as he often rejected my suggestions, there were times when I had to reject his. I remember one instance where I refused to change anything – it was a poem in dialogue form – because the words of the poem were true.

He replied: 'You can say to me that effectiveness is less than truth; I can only say that the truth must be made effectively true, and though every word of the truth be put down the result may well be a clot of truths.'

Soon after this he came to my house on a visit, and spent the whole evening finishing the poem 'Deaths and Entrances'. He had already done a complete version, but he was not satisfied with the ending which had originally had a hyena image. His exposition of the ending was elaborate and detailed. He did not write down, but he spoke, of all the accumulated forces of the projected words, and the weight they had to carry. I still have a work-sheet on which he jotted down some of the images which finally composed the last stanza, and it brings that particular evening to life more clearly than any photograph could have done.

At the end of 1941 I left for the Air Force. It was some time before I saw him again, but I still heard from him; and a year later he was sending me poems, as before. Then, early in 1943, I was moved to a station well within range of London, where Dylan now was; and I saw him regularly. At Chippenham he had worked on the first chapters of an unfinished novel, to be called 'Adventures in the Skin Trade', and he had collaborated with John Davenport in an extravagant literary thriller called 'Death of the King's Canary', which contained burlesques and parodies of living poets. Only one of the parodies was in fact written by Dylan, and this was the Empson one, which was printed in 'Horizon'.

Dylan now had a job making documentary films, and he was also writing scripts for broadcasting. I stayed with him frequently at his studio in Manresa Road. He hated being in his house if there were an air raid, but he did not mind the raid if he were in a pub. That is to say, he minded it terribly, but he felt he was in the right place. In the pubs he resented the smug talk he heard about the war, and he did not disguise his resentment. He was, wherever he recognized dishonesty or any form of Antichrist, the most aggressive pacifist I have ever seen. Being very courageous, he usually picked for his adversary anyone apparently physically formidable and strong, never a weak man.

The poems which now arrived at my Air Force station were about the war, and contained, to my mind, the most intense statements which had been made on it. Yet some were about Laugharne, and others were strictly religious poems. 'The Conversation of Prayer', 'A Refusal to Mourn the Death, by Fire, of a Child in London', and 'A Winter's Tale' all arrived in the same envelope. I was astonished by the two shorter poems, and I thought 'A Winter's Tale' the most beautiful long poem he had written. His own comment in the letter which came with the poems was that he thought the long one didn't come off, but he liked all of it.

There followed the sonnet, 'Among Those Killed in the Dawn Raid was A Man Aged A Hundred', 'Holy Spring', and the religious pattern-poem 'Vision and Prayer', in which the verses of the first part formed the shape of a diamond and the verses of the second part the shape of an hour-glass or prayer-wheel. The device was one that George Herbert had used, a poet whom Dylan particularly loved and admired. Yet the poem had found its original spur in the work of a very different poet. Dylan told me, when he was just beginning to write it, that he had read a most wonderful statement of Rilke about God being born in the next room. This must, I think, have been the poem, 'Du Nachbar Gott' from the Stundenbuch, which Dylan would have read in the translation of Babette Deutsch, published by New Directions. He knew Rilke before. At Laugharne Castle we had read the Duino Elegies together, taking it in turns to read one aloud, and they had moved him very much, even in translation; but he thought Rilke was 'a very odd boy indeed', although a great poet.

'Vision and Prayer' was rightly acclaimed as a fine religious poem. I had suggested to him that, although the words of the first part appeared to fit the diamond pattern organically, there were verses in the second part where the words seemed to have been drilled into position to fit the pattern of the prayer-wheel and that the line-endings did not coincide with the pauses of the voice, as they do, for instance, in Herbert's 'Easter Wings'. So I wondered whether he would consider trying out the second part in verses with lines of equal length. The suggestion did not appeal to Dylan at all. He had chipped out his poem with consummate care, working on it for months like an old carpenter, and he did not want to change it. He was right to stick to the pattern in which the poem was conceived, and I do not see now how he could have changed it without writing a different poem.

In September, 1944, came a new poem, of which the first line was familiar to me, and with it the note: 'Here is a new poem. It's a month and a bit premature. I do hope you like it, and would like very much to read it aloud to you. Will you read it aloud too? It's got, I think, a lovely slow lyrical movement.' And he added in a Postscript: 'In the poem, I notice, on copying out, that I have made October trees bare. I'll alter later.'

I opened the poem and read:

It was my thirtieth year to heaven
Woke to my hearing from harbour and neighbour wood
And the mussel pooled and the heron
Priested shore
The morning beckon
With water praying and call of seagull and rook
And the knock of sailing boats on the net webbed wall
Myself to set foot
That second
In the still sleeping town and set forth.

He did alter 'bare' to 'winged' trees in the second stanza and 'brown with October blood' (which was my only criticism) to 'leaved with October blood' in the last. It was the most beautiful poem he had made and one of the most beautiful, I think, in the language.

Dylan sent the poem from Llangain, near Carmarthen, and a few days later he and his family moved to New Quay to live. 'After Monday,' he wrote, 'our address will be Majoda, New Quay. The name is made of the beginnings of the names of the three children of the man who built the questionable house. I may alter the name to Catllewdylaer.'

From New Quay he still came to London quite often for broadcasts, which had become more frequent, and for his film work. We would meet Daniel Jones, who was in the army and at the very same place where I was, and Phil Lindsay, the historical novelist, and much of the time with them was spent doing composite poems to which each of us contributed a line. Dylan sometimes cheated and had more than one. Dan was a more lenient umpire and once, when I was not there, Dylan made a whole tiny poem for a child which ended

'And a little cruet flying in a cloud of jam'.

At New Quay Dylan wrote, among other scripts, 'Quite Early One Morning', which was the first sketch for 'Under Milk Wood'. His own name for the stories in 'Portrait of the Artist as a Young Dog' was 'illuminated reporting'; but in the broadcast scripts he carried this technique a stage further. They were denser than the stories, more packed with word-play, and each script involved a manipulation of words in which humour, colour, irony, exhilaration and pure verbal music were merged and adjusted to give the maximum effect of delight and surprise as well as to carry always the ring of truth. Perhaps the most ambitious was 'Return Journey' in which he described his return to blitzed Swansea after the war. This was written for different voices, with himself the narrator. I met him when he came to Swansea to check the order of the shops in the destroyed streets which were now a bare space.

'Deaths and Entrances' had been published over a year before this. I think it was Herbert Read who wrote: 'These poems cannot be reviewed. They can only be acclaimed.' It would be very difficult to think otherwise after such readings as Dylan himself gave of 'Fern Hill', 'Poem in October' and 'Ceremony After a Fire Raid'.

After 'Deaths and Entrances', Dylan had the idea of writing a single long poem to be called 'In Country Heaven', which would be published as a single book. It would be in several parts which would themselves be independent poems. He described in a talk the basic motif of this projected poem '... the poem becomes, at last, an affirmation of the beautiful and terrible worth of the Earth. It grows into a praise of what is and what could be on this lump in the skies. It is a poem about happiness.'

The first published part of this poem, called 'In Country Sleep' appeared in 'Horizon', badly misprinted, in 1947. This gave the title to the only new book of poems he was to publish before the 'Collected Poems' of 1952. It was printed in America by New Directions and contained six poems, the only six after 'Deaths and Entrances' he was to publish, except the 'Prologue' to the 'Collected Poems'. 'Once Below a Time', included in 'Collected Poems' but not in 'Deaths and Entrances' had been finished early in 1940. Besides 'In Country Sleep' were two other parts of the projected poem 'In Country Heaven', namely 'Over Sir John's Hill' and 'In the White Giant's Thigh'. There was also 'Lament', in ballad form, the long poem in assonance on his thirty-fifth birthday which seems to me to belong very much to the symbolism of 'In Country Heaven', and the moving Yeatsian poem for his father, written in the form of a villanelle: 'Do Not Go Gentle Into That Good Night'. These poems had already appeared in Europe in *Botteghe Oscure*.

For intricacy of construction and sureness of technique no better poems can be found in all Dylan's work than these last poems. There is even, throughout 'Over Sir John's Hill', a device of assonantal rhymes lengthening from the beginning to the end of each stanza which exactly corresponds to the images he is describing. I saw him in Laugharne when he had begun 'In the White Giant's Thigh' and he told me that he had spent three weeks working out the first line of that poem. When I last saw him, a week before he sailed to America, he said that there was no work in the world so hard as writing a poem. He had begun a new poem, an elegiac one, for his father who had died ten months before. He quoted a few lines to me, but he could not trust his memory and it was only a first outline. On that evening he described the libretto he proposed to do for the opera for Stravinsky whom he was to meet again, and collaborate with, after a few weeks of other work in New York. It bore a strong resemblance to the ideas of 'In Country Heaven'.

'Under Milk Wood' was finished just before he left. He had quoted a great deal of it to Daniel Jones and me at a cricket match in Swansea just after his return from a lecturing tour in America two or three years before. It was the culmination of all the scripts and of a certain part of the late poetry, too. It reminded me of a criticism he had once sent me of an early poem: 'You have rarified a motive: it should be made common.' In New York he was still revising 'Under Milk Wood' which was being staged there. He had said in July, when I spent a day with him in Laugharne, that although it was all right for the stage he was not finally satisfied with every detail of it for print.

Almost the last conversation Dylan had before his death was about the Garden of Eden. His wide recognition has always seemed to me marginal to the poetry. There are others who think of the poetry itself as marginal to his reputation, and some, with a reputation as critics themselves, who have said that in a few years there will be a change of heart, and that Dylan's reputation will suffer. It never seems to occur to them that to watch a poet's value on the literary Stock Exchange is the mark of a superficial mind, and it is not to such minds that these poems are addressed.

Research and Reperception

When a poet has finally chosen the words of a poem in the exact form in which he wants it given to the world, who, but he, can change it? The interest in what he has rejected has, for him in that moment, ceased to exist: it is scrubbed from the slate. Behind the finished poem lie the unfinished drafts, the labour that went into the poem before the final choice, before the moment which Yeats described as 'the poem coming together like the click of a box'. Yet, when such a rejected manuscript is seen, it exerts a particular fascination. It may even persuade the poet, at a later time, to alter his poem again.

The fascination of a succession of drafts towards a poem for the readers of a poet, those whom Dylan Thomas called 'the strangers' in the Preface to his 'Collected Poems', is more complex still. Yet, however deeply they are studied, I am not sure that more will ever come to light than the surface of the iceberg, so intricate and secret and unwritten is the progress of a poem. The research scholar who emerges with an apparently unassailable argument from such studies may lose his case to a single moment of memory from a witness, and may discover that the words of the finished poem alone, and ignorance of all that labour, would have been a better guide. Who would be the better for many versions of 'King Lear' or 'Hamlet'? The single line of accomplishment is worth all the matrix of alternatives.

I take at random an early poem of Dylan Thomas on which he spent five or six months. Dedicated to Caitlin, whom he had married a short time before its composition, it is the second poem in 'The Map of Love'. My first knowledge of this poem came from Dylan himself. He and his wife arrived at my house one day in the summer of 1937, and he recited to me the opening verse of the poem and a little of what followed. He had reached in composition the end of the third verse, the line:

Whalebed and bulldance, the gold bush of lions,

which was the followed by:

Proud as a mule's womb and huge as insects.

A week later he altered this second line. He had been seeking images of sterility and contrast, and it was on the beach below this cliff that he told me that, after much work on the line, he had changed it to:

Proud as a sucked stone and huge as sandgrains.

The change is interesting, not because 'sandgrains' had

been one of many suggested alternatives, but because the first rejected image was, like the sixth stanza of the poem, not then begun, linked with the fragment of a story, 'In the Direction of the Beginning', which he was writing and was to publish in *Wales* in March, 1938, after the poem to Caitlin was finished. This prose piece, the last to be written in the densely packed, symbol-charged, sexual, and sometimes surrealist style of the early stories, has two successive phrases:

> 'She raged in the mule's womb. She faltered in the galloping dynasty.'

The exploration of research and reperception of memory are different. I remember the excitement of hearing Dylan read 'In the Direction of the Beginning', the opening of what was to be the longest and best of all those stories, and the altogether different sensation of hearing him say, walking with me in Laugharne not many months later, that he would never write that kind of story again. The fragment remained a fragment: the story was never continued.

In all the early work there was a close link between poetry and prose, but a turning-point was now being reached, and the utter rejection of the style of the early prose came soon after the 'Poem to Caitlin' was finished, and this rejection was final.

Meanwhile the poem proceeded. The third line of the fourth verse was at first:

Her rude, red flight up cinder-nesting columns,

but 'rude, red tree' had been used in the very last line of the 'Altarwise by Owl-light' sonnet sequence; so Dylan, after some deliberation, changed this to 'molten'.

Not long after this Dylan told me that he had gone down into the tombs of Egypt and must come up in eight lines. He had reached the sixth verse. When he read me the opening line:

Ruin, the room of errors, one rood dropped

he said that he had first of all written: 'Ruin, the chamber of errors' and could not think what was wrong with the line. Then he had remembered. It was Madame Tussaud's Chamber of Horrors that had haunted him, and with a dropped 'h'. He was wonderfully amused by this: the grotesque, when it was so close to the true, always exhilarated him.

Of course the wonder he had experienced in reading about the opening of Tutankhamen's tomb is in this verse, and so, too, is the ninth sonnet of 'Altarwise by Owl-light', which ends:

This was the resurrection in the desert,
Death from a bandage, rants the mask of scholars
Gold on such features, and the linen spirit
Weds my long gentleman to dusts and furies;
With priest and pharaoh bed my gentle wound,
World in the sand, on the triangle landscape,
With stones of odyssey for ash and garland
And rivers of the dead around my neck.

And here is the sixth verse of 'Poem to Caitlin':

> Ruin, the room of errors, one rood dropped
> Down the stacked sea and water-pillared shade,
> Weighed in rock shroud, is my proud pyramid;
> Where, wound in emerald linen and sharp wind,
> The hero's head lies scraped of every legend,
> Comes love's anatomist with sun-gloved hand
> Who picks the live heart on a diamond.

After a couple of months on this coast Dylan went to Ringwood, in Dorset, where the poem was finished in the house of Caitlin's mother. His progress towards the final revision is indicated in the letter dated 13th November, 1937, which came to me with the poem:

'...Lines 4 & 5 of the last verse might, perhaps, sound too fluent: I mean, they might sound as though they came too easily in a manner I have done my best to discard, but they say exactly what I mean them to. Are they clear? Once upon a time, before my death and resurrection, before the 'terrible' world had shown itself to me (however lyingly, as lines 6 & 7 of the last verse might indicate) as not so terrible after all, a wind had blown that had frightened everything and created the first ice and frost by frightening the falling snow so much that the blood of each flake froze. This is probably clear, but, even to me, the lines skip (almost) along so that they are taken too quickly, and then mainly by the eye.'[1]

[1] 'Letters to Vernon Watkins' (Dent & Faber 1957, pp.30.31)

In my reply I suggested that the last verse bore marks of hurry, of impatient composition, in spite of the slow gestation of the poem; and only a week after Dylan's first letter came a second, saying:

'I agree with you entirely as to the (apparently) hurried ending of my sixty-line-year's work, and will alter the middle lines of the last verse.'[2]

I have not the alternative drafts of this poem. All I write, I write from memory, concerning its changes. I remember also one earlier line in the poem as forming the climax of a different composition, on a separate work-sheet. Dylan Thomas always knew what he wanted, but he did not always find immediately its true and final place. A significant example of this is the last line of his birthday poem, 'Twenty-Four Years', where at last the true place was found for what had been written long before.

However laborious the evidence of a poem's making, composition is always a swift, lightning thing. The vital leap that connects one part of a poem to another is only partly shadowed in the drafts. Research belongs to time, but reperception belongs to the source of the poem, which may be defined as time's arrested moment. Yeats has described, in 'Lapis Lazuli', the poet's toil, even his tragic toil, as all belonging to joy, to what is gay:

All things fall and are built again
And those that build them again are gay.

[2] Ibid., p.32

Nor can the research worker ever afford to forget Blake's words:

He who bends to himself a Joy
Doth the winged life destroy;
But he who kisses the Joy as it flies
Lives in Eternity's sunrise.

Vernon Watkins April 1963

Eight Poems by Dylan Thomas

My real concern is with the poems as Dylan Thomas handled them in preparing his final version, the version which now stands in his 'Collected Poems'. I am less concerned with the first genesis of the poem, which in these poems, as in many others, may be traced back to drafts in his early Notebooks, written at a time before I first knew him. I did not meet Dylan Thomas until he was twenty. A detailed examination of the notebooks brings many things to light. I remember looking through the preliminary drafts of his poems in the British Museum, feeling, indeed, very sceptical as I turned over the first pages, until I suddenly came on the first jottings for 'After the Funeral'. These excited me, but not nearly so much as my first acquaintance with the poem in 1938, when Dylan had suddenly reached maturity, both in verse and prose, beyond anything he had achieved before. Of the eight poems I am going to discuss the first is 'After the Funeral'.

This poem began with twenty-five lines in the February 1933 Notebook, where, as Professor Ralph Maud points out in his careful examination of texts, 'Entrances in Dylan Thomas's Poetry', it is not about any specific person. 'On the death of his aunt,' Maud writes, 'Thomas turned the poem into a personal elegy.' This does not, for me, in any way invalidate the poem as an elegy for Ann Jones throughout, so deeply I trust the second phase of composition, what I call 'the second pressure', often more creative than the first. For me the true genesis of the poem is in the opening part which I received from Dylan with a letter in March, 1938. It arrived as a fifteen-line poem, ending with the line:

> Round the parched worlds of Wales and drowned
> each sun.

I had not seen a word of this poem before, and I wrote back to say how very much I liked it; and in April, in a rush of verse, he extended it. We discussed the poem, which seemed to me the finest he had written up to that moment. It was the first poem to which he gave a title, for in its first printing in 'Life and Letters To-Day' in the Summer of 1938 it appeared under the title, 'In Memory of Ann Jones'. This was not the only way in which it was unique among the poems Dylan wrote up to his twenty-fourth year. It was the first poem about a person. There had been poems addressed and dedicated to a person, but this was about one. It was a religious poem written from the outside of another person's religious faith, a narrower faith than his own. That person was his favourite aunt, the eldest of his mother's sisters, married to a tenant farmer, Jack Jones. She is the aunt of his story 'The Peaches', which was also published in 'Life and Letters To-Day' and became the first of the stories in 'Portrait of the Artist as a Young Dog'. She lived in the farmhouse at Fern Hill, above Laugharne, where Dylan stayed so often as a child, and which he remembers so clearly in his poem 'Fern Hill'.

Before the poem 'After the Funeral' was finished, it went through a number of revisions. Dylan altered line five from 'The spittled eyes, the salt ponds in the sleeves' to 'The spittled eyes, the stiff lakes in the sleeves', but I persuaded him to change it back. The whole of the second part of the poem, after the five beautiful bracketed lines of its centre, is an unfolding of contrasts, the contrast beginning with his own bardic prominence as funeral orator and her silent humility, 'her wood-tongued virtue', for a bell with a wooden clapper would produce least sound. Another contrast: 'this monumental Argument of the hewn voice' was altered to 'this monumental Argument of the small voice', but afterwards altered back. Also 'cloud-stained, marble hands', which he originally had, immediately before this, was altered to 'cloud-sopped, marble hands', unfortunately misprinted in Life and Letters Today as 'cloud-sapped'. Dylan chose 'cloud-sopped' because he wanted the exaltation of cloudy images, especially, I think, as represented in religious paintings, and the hard scrubbing of her domestic life, in a single word. The greatest improvement of all in the final revision was made in the following line, where 'gesture and psalm' had been used as verbs, followed by: 'To me forever over her grave until'. 'Storm me forever' did the trick, and gesture and psalm went into their right parenthetical place.

This poem has the only surrealist image that I can find in the whole of Dylan's poetry in the lines:

> Shakes a desolate boy who slits his throat
> In the dark of the coffin and sheds dry leaves.

Surrealism may be found in that quarry of the early stories, from which many of the early poems were struck, but it did not appear in the verse.

There is also, in the ending, a reminiscence of a passage in Djuna Barnes' novel 'Nightwood', which Dylan had been reading at this time, and which he greatly admired. I mean the line:

> The stuffed lung of the fox twitch and cry Love.

Here is the passage in 'Nightwood':

> 'I tell you, Madame, if one gave birth to a heart on a plate, it would say "Love" and twitch like the lopped leg of a frog'.

I come now to the poem Dylan Thomas wrote for his twenty-fourth birthday, the last poem in his third book, 'The Map of Love', comprising sixteen poems and seven stories. Here it is:

TWENTY-FOUR YEARS

Twenty-four years remind the tears of my eyes.
(Bury the dead for fear that they walk to the grave in labour.)
In the groin of the natural doorway I crouched like a tailor
Sewing a shroud for the journey
By the light of the meat-eating sun.
Dressed to die, the sensual strut begun,
With my red veins full of money,
In the final direction of the elementary town
I advance for as long as forever is.

Dylan Thomas was born on October 27th, 1914, and this poem was sent to me on a postcard in October, 1938. Around the poem, in his minute handwriting, was an explanatory note:

'This very short poem is for my birthday just arriving. I know you'll hate the use of the "Forever" line, but there it is. I scrapped the poem beginning with that line long ago, and at last – I think – I've found the inevitable place for it: it was a time finding that place... In the first version I had "like a stuffed tailor". I think stuffed is wrong, don't you? Try to read the end of the poem as though you didn't know the lines. I do feel they're right. In the old "Forever" poem they were completely out of place – & the rest of the poem wouldn't stand without them. So bang went the whole poem, obviously, & here at last is what it should be.'

This note does, I think, illustrate one characteristic of Dylan's method of composition. He was acutely self-critical and ready to scrap a poem which did not meet his own exact demands; but if a phrase came to him which was central in his imagination he did not discard it; it would, at an unpredictable moment, perhaps many years later, find its way into a poem. In this case the line

For as long as forever is

had been the opening line of a poem written while he still lived in Swansea, a poem full of images taken from hunting. Ducks, hares and foxes were in the poem, so far as I can remember, from his once reading the first three stanzas of that unfinished poem aloud to me. There were either two or three finished stanzas, and the last line of the first had been:

Forever the hunted world at a snail's gallop goes.

Far from hating the use of the 'Forever' line in the birthday poem, I found it, and the whole poem, the most moving thing he had sent me. My only disagreement at that time was over the inclusion of the second, bracketed line:

(Bury the dead for fear that they walk to the grave in labour.)

I now think I was wrong in suggesting that that line belonged more to Shakespeare than to that particular poem, I do not mean as a plagiarism, but in point of style. I think it right that a more ancient voice than the poet's should support the truth in a poem. Also I feel that the line belongs to Dylan's poem and that it enhances the beauty of what follows it. My only criticism of it is that another poet might have written it, which is not true of any of the other lines; but I no longer think this criticism is valid. The parts of a poem need not always justify themselves by originality; they are justified by *being* there. I had suggested omitting the line, but I now realise that the poem would be incomplete without it, not only because it is an assonantal rhyme with 'tailor' at the end of the next line, but because it is the initial weight that drives the poem forward.

Dylan called his poems 'statements on the way to the grave', and this is an even clearer statement of faith than the poem 'Once it was the Colour of Saying' which was to follow it. It meant the end of the early, symbol-charged stories, and the beginning of the new style of prose which was to find its fullest development in the late broadcast scripts and in 'Under Milk Wood'. He now cared for human beings for themselves, and not as figures in a boy's dream, not as puppets and extensions of his own unfolding adolescence.

But the poem which really announced the new style is 'Once it was the Colour of Saying', a poem whose first four lines were held up to ridicule by Beachcomber in his comic column in the Daily Express. It was not the only time that Dylan recognized the homage of a sneer.

I really think that this little poem, written in 1938, marks the turning-point in Dylan Thomas's work, after which he was unable and unwilling to write in his early manner. It is the equivalent of Yeats' poem 'A Coat' in which *he* announced the bare style of his later poetry and the death of his early, ornate style:

A COAT

I made my song a coat
Covered with embroideries
Out of old mythologies
From heel to throat;
But the fools caught it,
Wore it in the world's eyes
As though they'd wrought it.
Song, let them take it
For there's more enterprise
In walking naked.

Here now is Dylan Thomas' poem:

ONCE IT WAS THE COLOUR OF SAYING

Once it was the colour of saying
Soaked my table the uglier side of a hill
With a capsized field where a school sat still
And a black and white patch of girls grew playing;
The gentle seaslides of saying I must undo
That all the charmingly drowned arise to cockcrow
    and kill.
When I whistled with mitching boys through a
    reservoir park
Where at night we stoned the cold and cuckoo
Lovers in the dirt of their leafy beds,
The shade of their trees was a word of many shades
And a lamp of lightning for the poor in the dark;
Now my saying shall be my undoing,
And every stone I wind off like a reel.

In this poem, as in THEN WAS MY NEOPHYTE, and

again in the long poem HOW SHALL MY ANIMAL, Dylan imagines the sea as the element of composition, of prophecy, of life's vision and symbolic interpretation, a kind of film-mechanism against which he rebelled. Just as in THEN WAS MY NEOPHYTE 'the winder of the clockwise scene' like this:

He films my vanity,
Shot in the wind by tilted arcs,
Over the water come
Children from homes and children's parks
Who speak on a finger and thumb,
And the masked, headless boy.
His reels and mystery
The winder of the clockwise scene
Wound like a ball of lakes
Then threw on that tide-hoisted screen
Love's image till my heartbone breaks
By a dramatic sea.

So, in ONCE IT WAS THE COLOUR OF SAYING he rebels against his own 'sea-slides of saying' which he must 'undo', as they belong to the under-water symbolic world of his early work, and not to the real world of the work which was to come. Yet this poem is very condensed, very complex. It is a composite statement with separate levels of interpretation. First of all, it is a very exact description of Dylan's work-room in the house at the top of Cwmdonkin Drive where he lived with his parents. I used to go there regularly at one time, especially on Saturday afternoons. His table was in front of a big bay-window facing West above the steep hill. Opposite were grass and trees, but I think he calls this 'the uglier side of the hill' because it misses the view over Swansea Bay and the docks which were on the East side. Above the hill was Cwmdonkin Park, with its large reservoir. The 'zoo of the willow-groves' has been cut down. The bandstand has gone, and in those days swans drifted in the water... Halfway down the hill, on the other side of the road, was a small playing-field, 'cap-sized' as he describes it, only about quarter of the size of a real one, where girls, dressed in black and white, came to practice hockey; capsized, too, on the sea of his imagination and the reservoir park of his childhood. 'Where a school sat still' refers to the deaf-and-dumb school, also just at the top of the hill, the same building that haunts the NEOPHYTE lines:

Children from homes and children's parks
Who speak on a finger and thumb.

The hill itself is parallel to Mount Pleasant Hill, on which the old Grammar School stood, where Dylan was the editor of the school magazine, and from which he would mitch with other boys to go into the park.

That is only one level of interpretation. The poem is also the abandonment of a way of looking and a way of writing – even of a way of throwing stones. In a sense everything he had attacked and caricatured has become sacred. The time was the Autumn of 1938. Dylan's subjective stories, full of symbols and influenced by surrealism, had reached their climax in the most ambitious story of all, IN THE DIRECTION OF THE BEGINNING, which he was never to finish. I remember him remarking to me, when I said how much I admired its opening, that he would never write that kind of story again. He said it with great emphasis. He would now write about real people in his prose, and his verse would move in the direction of the living voice.

A SAINT ABOUT TO FALL

Just at this time, and it was the time of Munich and the imminence of war, Dylan was working on a much longer poem. It was the first of two birth poems printed at the end of THE MAP OF LOVE before the final poem, TWENTY-FOUR YEARS. The second of these two poems was to be a dialogue between an unborn child and its mother, and it was about this that Robert Graves, who has so many children but doesn't seem to know how they are born, showed such ignorance and obtuseness in his Clark lecture. However, it is the first poem that concerns me now. A SAINT ABOUT TO FALL was first printed in 'Poetry (London)' under the title POEM IN THE NINTH MONTH. He recited its first stanza to me when he came to my house in the late summer of 1938, but it was not until December that it was finished.

Caitlin Thomas was expecting her first child in January, and Dylan expected war to break out even before he became a father. As it happened, war was not to break out until a week after the publication of THE MAP OF LOVE.

The poem is in three stanzas. The scenery of the poem is Laugharne, the Carmarthenshire fishing-village where Dylan and Caitlin had gone to live soon after their marriage. The first stanza, about the actual moment of a child's falling into birth, is full of exaltation and mystery.

The second brings heaven down to earth; and the third sets against the imminence and lunacy of war the exaltation and validity of birth. The reality of birth is presented with great violence, and the new-born child is declared holy and full of joy in spite of all the unholy and unjoyful circumstances awaiting him. He is presented in the last stanza as stronger than all the opposing forces. As Dylan said to me in the letter accompanying the finished poem: the most important words are 'Cry joy' at the end. And following these words is a magical punning use of the word 'second' to create the compound mystery of birth.

The first stanza, is the moment before birth: In the second stanza the new situation is presented:

> Glory cracked like a flea.

The third stanza opens with images of lunacy and war and ends with the moment of birth:

> Strike in the time-bomb town,
> Raise the live rafters of the eardrum,
> Throw your fear a parcel of stone
> Through the dark asylum...
>
> And makes with a flick of the thumb and sun
> A thundering bullring of your silent and girl-circled
> island.

Dylan sent all the poems of the MAP OF LOVE to me as they were finished; and throughout the war he continued to send me poems, most of those in DEATHS AND ENTRANCES coming singly, but sometimes two or three at a time. Of all these I think perhaps the most beautiful is the one I opened in September, 1944, again with Carmarthenshire scenery, but perceived also through his own childhood. Laugharne harbour, the farmhouse and wood at Fern Hill and the hilltop church are all in the poem. He was on the point of leaving Carmarthen when he sent it, to live in New Quay, in Cardigan. The poem is called POEM IN OCTOBER and here is the note which accompanied it:

'...Here is a new poem. It's a month and a bit premature. I do hope you like it, and wd like very much to read it aloud to you. Will you read it aloud too? It's got, I think, a lovely slow lyrical movement.' And he added a Postscript:

'In the poem, I notice, on copying out, that I have made October trees bare. I'll alter later.'

I opened the poem and read:

It was my thirtieth year to heaven
Woke to my hearing from harbour and neighbour wood
And the mussel pooled and the heron
Priested shore
The morning beckon
With water praying and call of seagull and rook
And the knock of sailing boats on the net webbed wall
Myself to set foot
That second
In the still sleeping town and set forth.

My birthday began with the water
Birds and the birds of the bare trees flying my name
Above the farms and the white horses
And I rose
In rainy autumn
And walked abroad in a shower of all my days.
High tide and the heron dived when I took the road
Over the border
And the gates
Of the town closed as the town awoke.

A springful of larks in a rolling
Cloud and the roadside bushes brimming with whistling
Blackbirds and the sun of October
Summery
On the hill's shoulder,
Here were fond climates and sweet singers suddenly
Come in the morning where I wandered and listened
To the rain wringing
Wind blow cold
In the wood faraway under me.

Pale rain over the dwindling harbour
And over the sea wet church the size of a snail
With its horns through mist and the castle
Brown as owls
But all the gardens
Of spring and summer were blooming in the tall tales
Beyond the border and under the lark full cloud.
There could I marvel
My birthday
Away but the weather turned around.

It turned away from the blithe country
And down the other air and the blue altered sky
Streamed again a wonder of summer
With apples
Pears and red currants
And I saw in the turning so clearly a child's
Forgotten mornings when he walked with his mother
Through the parables
Of sun light
And the legends of the green chapels

And the twice told fields of infancy
That his tears burned my cheeks and his heart moved in mine.
These were the woods the river and sea
Where a boy
In the listening
Summertime of the dead whispered the truth of his joy
To the trees and the stones and the fish in the tide.
And the mystery
Sang alive
Still in the water and singingbirds.

And there I could marvel my birthday
Away but the weather turned around. And the true
Joy of the long dead child sang burning
In the sun.
It was my thirtieth
Year to heaven stood there in the summer noon
Though the town below was brown with October blood.
O may my heart's truth
Still be sung
On this high hill in a year's turning.

He did, afterwards, alter 'bare' to 'winged' trees in the second stanza and 'brown with October blood' to 'leaved with October blood' in the last.

This more than any other poem in DEATHS AND ENTRANCES', except possibly A WINTER'S TALE', is the forerunner of IN COUNTRY SLEEP, the title poem of his next book, published in America in 1952. Before leaving it, there are one or two things I should say. A poem is made permanent by the magic which comes to the poet in the course of composition, but one should not underestimate the laborious preparation for that possibility. The first of Dylan's entirely assonantal poems was THERE WAS A SAVIOUR, a poem about invasion which he finished at the beginning of 1940. He was exploring the rewards of rhyming with vowel-sounds only, because, as he told me once, he disliked having rhymes stamped ready for him like the stations on railway tickets. Gradually he evolved stanza forms to fit his assonantal pattern, and sometimes, where necessary, he used rhyme, too. The pattern in IT WAS MY THIRTIETH YEAR TO HEAVEN is not absolutely regular, but where it is broken it is broken with genius. The result is, to my ear, an intuitively perfect poem.

The easy, and apparently effortless utterance is, of course, deceptive. More than a hundred drafts were made, and the poem was begun in his mind much earlier, as I remember him saying to me: 'I know the beginning of my next poem. It is going to be:

It was my twenty-seventh year to heaven.

The book DEATHS AND ENTRANCES, for which this and FERN HILL were two of the last poems to be written, was published in 1946. In the remaining seven years before his death he was to finish only seven more poems, but they are the culmination of his achievement.

After DEATHS AND ENTRANCES Dylan planned to write a single long poem in parts, each part being a separate poem. This long poem was to be called IN COUNTRY HEAVEN; and its plan was expounded in a broadcast talk in which he read the three parts he had finished, the poems called IN COUNTRY SLEEP, OVER SIR JOHN'S HILL, and IN THE WHITE GIANT'S THIGH. This is what he said:

'The poem is to be called "In Country Heaven". The godhead, the author, the milky-way farmer, the first cause, architect, lamp-lighter, quintessence, the beginning Word, the anthropomorphic bawler-out and blackballer, the stuff of all men, scapegoat, martyr, maker, woe-bearer – He, on top of a hill in heaven, weeps whenever, outside that state of being called his country, one of his worlds drops dead, vanishes screaming, shrivels, explodes, murders itself. And, when He weeps, Light and His tears slide down together, hand in hand. So, at the beginning of the projected poem, He weeps, and Country Heaven is suddenly dark. Bushes and owls blow out like candles. And the countrymen of heaven crouch all together under the hedges and, among themselves in the tear-salt darkness, surmise which world, which star, which of their late, turning homes in the skies, has gone for ever. And this time, spreads the heavenly hedgerow rumour, it is the Earth. The Earth has killed itself. It is black, petrified, wizened, poisoned, burst; insanity has blown it rotten;

and no creatures at all, joyful, despairing, cruel, kind, dumb, afire, loving, dull, shortly and brutishly hunt their days down like enemies on that corrupted face. And, one by one, those heavenly hedgerow-men who were once of the Earth call to one another, through the long night – Light and His tears falling, what they remember, what they sense in the submerged wilderness and on the exposed hair's breadth of the mind, what they feel trembling on the nerves of a nerve, what they know in their Edenic hearts, of that self-called place. They remember places, fears, loves, exultation, misery, animal joy, ignorance, and mysteries, all *we* know and do not know.

The poem is made of these tellings. And the poem becomes, at last, an affirmation of the beautiful and terrible worth of the Earth. It grows into a praise of what is and what could be on this lump in the skies. It is a poem about happiness.'

This exposition is not unlike the subject of the opera which Dylan planned to make with Stravinsky. He was in New York in October, 1953, revising and rehearsing the stage version of UNDER MILK WOOD and was due to leave for Hollywood to join Stravinsky when he became ill. Stravinsky describes in his memoirs how he received a telegram which he thought would announce his friend's arrival; when he opened it, it announced that he was dead. The opera on which they would have collaborated was to describe the holiness of Earth which had been devastated, leaving alive only one old man and his children. Visitors from another planet would come to take the children away; and the old man, who alone remembered the beauty and mystery of Earth, would try to describe them to the visitors and his children, who had been too young to know these things. He would describe what leaves were like, and grass. Dylan made, I think, a draft of this libretto; but I remember it only from his own description, a very short time before he left for America, on the last evening I spent with him. Dylan made also two or three fragmentary drafts of the poem IN COUNTRY HEAVEN, written in entirely assonantal form.

I come next to OVER SIR JOHN'S HILL, one of the three finished poems belonging to IN COUNTRY HEAVEN', written in 1949. It is, I think, the most perfect in form of all Dylan's poems, in its combined use of rhyme and assonance. The scenery is again Laugharne, Sir John's hill being the big hill West of the Boat House, overlooking the estuary. The poem is in five stanzas, and in each stanza there are, at the end of long lines, three feminine assonantal rhymes. In each case the second of these is slightly longer than the first, and the third slightly longer than the second:

heron; hedges; headstone.
paddles; passage; prancing.
dilly; dingle; distant.
whistles; windows; whispering;
scaly; shaken; sailing.

I mention this only to show how intricate the musical structure of the poem is. There is an equally exact control and judgment in the short lines.

Some have suggested that in the line from the nursery rhyme: 'dilly dilly' Dylan was punning on his own name.

That is possible. But it is utterly wrong to read 'Fishing in the tear of the Towy' in the last stanza as 'Fishing in the tear (tare) of the Towy'. I once heard that mistake made by an actor on the wireless. How, I wonder, did he reconcile this to 'the tune of the slow wear-willow river' at the end of the last stanza?

In the poem the holy hawk is taken as the instrument of God's destructive will, and the heron, which haunts all these last poems, as the meditative and grieving witness of the small birds on which the hawk preys. The mountain itself is the judge of God's mercy and their fate.

OVER SIR JOHN'S HILL and DO NOT GO GENTLE INTO THAT GOOD NIGHT. Dylan Thomas's writing of this and other poems for IN COUNTRY HEAVEN was interrupted by many things, but chiefly by his work on UNDER MILK WOOD. A little after his writing of the three finished parts, I mean the three parts which are called IN COUNTRY SLEEP, OVER SIR JOHN'S HILL, and IN THE WHITE GIANT'S THIGH, his father became very ill and was also threatened with blindness. It was then that Dylan wrote the poem DO NOT GO GENTLE INTO THAT GOOD NIGHT'. In his COLLECTED POEMS this poem is not in chronological order, as it took the place of the short and light poem PAPER AND STICKS which was in DEATHS AND ENTRANCES but which he left out from the COLLECTED POEMS after seeing it in the proof copy. It was the only poem from his published books that he rejected.

Just as OVER SIR JOHN'S HILL can be better understood after seeing Laugharne, DO NOT GO GENTLE INTO THAT GOOD NIGHT can be better understood by knowing what

Dylan's father was like. A great reader of Shakespeare, with a magnificent voice which Dylan inherited, he was the very opposite of Dylan in his social life, misanthropic, disillusioned, fiercely pessimistic, hating grass and the countryside where he lived, and particularly loathing commonplaces about the weather. His own were different. When it was raining he said: 'His work'. Later he would say: 'The sun has come out again. What foolishness!' At the end of his life, when he was seventy and ill, he began to be less savage, more benign; then he fell critically ill, and even when he was half blind and likely to die, the old indignation which Dylan loved did not return. Stravinsky, who set the poem to music, made the mistake of thinking that it was written after his father's death. In the dedication of this memorial to Dylan he said so; but Dylan's father did not die until some eighteen months later, less than a year before Dylan himself.

Other mistakes have been made over the poem, the worst being the misprinting of its fifth line in many editions of the COLLECTED POEMS, where 'had forked no lightning' which is correct, and which was correctly printed in IN COUNTRY SLEEP, was misprinted as either '*has* forked no lightning' or '*have* forked no lightning'. I have seen both errors. The latest editions of COLLECTED POEMS have put this right, but for anyone in doubt it is only necessary to listen to Dylan's own recording of his poem by Caedmon.

The poem is the only example of a Villanelle in all Dylan's poetry. He did use strict French forms two or three times. But only for individual friends, and the only published example I can think of is his nine-line parody of William Empson REQUEST TO LEDA, which came out in *Horizon*, but this is really nothing more than a light exercise. He was immensely amused when Empson took it seriously.

Of all Dylan's poems DO NOT GO GENTLE is the closest in language to the later Yeats, and it is his triumph that, in spite of this, it is entirely his own poem. Nor could anyone but Dylan have created out of a colloquial expression a line of such metaphysical range and depth as the first. In the last verse I find for myself a reminiscence of Kierkegaard, a kind of transposition of Kierkegaard's learning that his father had once stood upon a hill and cursed God. But such a reminiscence is only one dimension of the poem's effect, just as the knowledge of Dylan's father's indignation and of his threatened blindness, and of his sinking into a more benign state, is only another.

> Do not go gentle into that good night,
> Old age should burn and rave at close of day;
> Rage, rage against the dying of the light.
>
> Though wise men at their end know dark is right,
> Because their words had forked no lightning they
> Do not go gentle into that good night.
>
> Good men, the last wave by, crying how bright
> Their frail deeds might have danced in a green bay,
> Rage, rage against the dying of the light.
>
> Wild men who caught and sang the sun in flight,
> And learn, too late, they grieved it on its way,
> Do not go gentle into that good night.

Grave men, near death, who see with blinding sight
Blind eyes could blaze like meteors and be gay,
Rage, rage against the dying of the light.

And you, my father, there on the sad height,
Curse, bless me now with your fierce tears, I pray.
Do not go gentle into that good night.
Rage, rage against the dying of the light.

Elegy

I come now, last of all, to the 'Elegy' for his father which Dylan did not live to finish. I remember him in Laugharne quoting to me the first line of 'In the White Giant's Thigh', only a part of which was then written, and saying that this line had taken him three weeks to get right. But it was in Swansea in the Summer of 1953 that he recited to me the opening lines of the 'Elegy', which I remembered when I was shown the variants of these lines several years after his death. I was shown, first of all, a single sheet of paper; and then, about six months later, on the very morning after I had spent a month copying his letters, the notebook and papers of all the drafts towards this poem were put into my hands. They showed once more how laborious was the writing of each of these last poems. There were more than sixty pages of drafts and marginal lines and repeated transcriptions of the opening lines. Approximately the first seventeen lines were completed, but these had many variants, and the title itself was TOO PROUD TO DIE on some of the sheets and ELEGY on what seemed to me to be the latest versions.

My first attempt to complete the poem failed, but I was helped by two things: Dylan's own prose note which he made for composition, and the fact that I had read nothing but his own poetry and letters for a month. The result is the poem which I am now going to read.

The poem is closely linked with DO NOT GO GENTLE INTO THAT GOOD NIGHT, but is more ambitious, both in theme and in the handling of language. I have made clear the point which Dylan reached in composition by bracketing the added lines. All but a few of these added lines occur somewhere in his rough drafts, but not at all in the order in which I have used them, though several pairs of lines are in sequence. The five lines preceding the brackets had a great many variants and were selected from different versions. One had 'In the crouching town', and another had 'monkey hand', and so on. The lines about the hand, which were a statement of fact, as Dylan had held his father's hand while he died, were the point he had reached in the body of the poem, but the other lines scattered through sixty pages were sufficient to make a coherent whole. The actual form of the poem, which is composed in quatrains, remained a problem, as in one of the two most complete versions it was set out in continuous lines, without a verse break, and in the other in separate verses of three lines each. It was the latter form that I chose. Dylan had the same hesitation over IN THE WHITE GIANT'S THIGH, which, also composed in quatrains, did not match the verse break to the rhyming structure but placed it where his imagination wanted a longer pause in the poem. What he sought, in these very last poems, was the concealment of technical structure behind the imaginative effect. Fundamentally the lay-out of a poem does not matter, except as an indication of voice-pause, and

I think this a small consideration; but I also think Dylan would have chosen the pattern of the three-lined verses for the printing of ELEGY.

ELEGY

Too proud to die, broken and blind he died
The darkest way, and did not turn away,
A cold kind man brave in his narrow pride

On that darkest day. Oh, forever may
He lie lightly, at last, on the last, crossed
Hill, under the grass, in love, and there grow

Young among the long flocks, and never lie lost
Or still all the numberless days of his death, though
Above all he longed for his mother's breast

Which was rest and dust, and in the kind ground
The darkest justice of death, blind and unblessed.
Let him find no rest but be fathered and found,

I prayed in the crouching room, by his blind bed,
In the muted house, one minute before
Noon, and night, and light. The rivers of the dead

Veined his poor hand I held, and I saw
Through his unseeing eyes to the roots of the sea.
[An old tormented man three-quarters blind,

I am not too proud to cry that He and he
Will never never go out of my mind.
All his bones crying, and poor in all but pain,

Being innocent, he dreaded that he died
Hating his God, but what he was was plain:
An old kind man brave in his burning pride.

The sticks of the house were his; his books he owned.
Even as a baby he had never cried;
Nor did he now, save to his secret wound.

Out of his eyes I saw the last light glide.
Here among the light of the lording sky
An old blind man is with me where I go

Walking in the meadows of his son's eye
On whom a world of ills came down like snow.
He cried as he died, fearing at last the spheres'

Last sound, the world going out without a breath:
Too proud to cry, too frail to check the tears,
And caught between two nights, blindness and death.

O deepest wound of all that he should die
On that darkest day. Oh, he could hide
The tears out of his eyes, too proud to cry.

Until I die he will not leave my side.]

NOTE

This unfinished Elegy of Dylan Thomas was given the title 'Elegy' in the latest version of the poem after the provisional titles 'The Darkest Way' or 'Too Proud to Die' had been used in preparatory drafts. Among his papers he left sixty pages of manuscript work towards the poem, including this note:

1. Although he was too proud to die, he *did* die, blind, in the most agonizing way but he did not flinch from death and was brave in his pride.
2. In his innocence, and thinking he was God-hating, he never knew that what he was: an old kind man in his burning pride.
3. Now he will not leave my side, though he is dead.
4. His mother said that as a baby he never cried; nor did he, as an old man; he just cried to his secret wound & his blindness, never aloud.

The rest of the manuscript work consists of phrases, lines, couplets, and line-endings, and transcripts of the poems in various degrees of completeness. The two most complete versions, which are clearly the latest, are both written in quatrains. One, with no title, has no division into verses, and the second, with the title 'Elegy' is divided into verses of three lines. This, to me, seems to be the latest version of all, and seems to hold the final form the poem was to take. The poem extends to the seventeenth line, ending 'to the roots of the sea', after which there is a line which is deleted.

The extension of the poem has been built up from the manuscript notes. The lines are all found there, except that two or three have been adjusted to fit the rhyming scheme. 'Breath' was an isolated marginal word which I have used in line thirty-four; and 'plain', which ends line twenty-three, has been added to 'was' without justification from the manuscript. In the third line I have chosen 'narrow pride' as against 'burning pride' although 'burning' occurs more often than 'narrow' in the transcripts; bit it was 'narrow' in that line that he quoted to me from memory when I last saw him.

Of the added lines sixteen are exactly as Dylan Thomas wrote them, and the remainder are only altered to the extent of an inversion of one or two words. Their order might well have been different. The poem might also have been made much longer. It recalls the earlier poem, also written for his father: 'Do Not Go Gentle Into That Good Night', but it is clear that in this last poem Dylan Thomas was attempting something even more immediate and more difficult.

Note on
'In Country Heaven'

When Dylan Thomas died, his long poem 'In Country Heaven' was left incomplete. The projected poem, as expounded in a broadcast talk produced by Douglas Cleverdon on the Third Programme on September 25th, 1950, and printed in the collection 'Quite Early One Morning' (Dent, 1954), was to have comprised several parts, each an independent poem, and of these only three: 'In Country Sleep', 'Over Sir John's Hill' and 'In The White Giant's Thigh', were completed. A fourth poem with the same title as the whole work was conceived as one of these parts, but until several years after his death I did not believe he had written a single line of this. Then I was quite unexpectedly shown the copy of a draft towards the poem. This, a fragmentary version, beset by alternatives, is, I am told, in the possession of Mr T. E. Hanley of Bradford, Pennsylvania, and it is almost certainly the earlier of the two in existence. The second was given by Dylan Thomas to John Malcolm Brinnin. It is more resolved, and carries only a suggested alternative in line 13, and an underlined word 'blackamoor' in line 24 which might indicate a return to 'negro' in Dylan Thomas's mind. The last line of all in the composition:

Young Aesop fabling by the coracled Towy

is separated from the two preceding lines by a space, but it conforms to his pattern for a third line.

Here is the poem:

IN COUNTRY HEAVEN

I.

Always when he, in Country Heaven,
(Whom my heart hears),
Crosses the breast of the praising East, and kneels,
Humble in all his planets,
And weeps on the abasing hill,

Then in the delight and groves of beasts and birds
And the canonized valley
Where the downfall stars sing grazing still
And the angels whirr like pheasants
Through aisles of leaves,

Light and his tears glide down together
(O hand in hand)
From the country eyes, salt and sun, star and woe
Down the cheek bones and whinnying
Downs into the low browsing dark.

Doused in hamlets of heaven swing the loft lamps,
In the black buried spinneys
Bushes and owls blow out like a spark,
And the seraphic fields of shepherds
Fade with their rose-

White, God's bright, flocks, the belled lambs leaping,
(His gentle kind);
The shooting star hawk locked blind in a lame cloud
Over the blackamoor shires
Hears the belfries and the cobbles

Of the twelve apostles' towns ring in his night;
And the long fox like fire
Prowls flaming among the cockerels
In the plunged farms of heaven's keeping,
But they sleep sound.

For the fifth element is pity,
(Pity for death);
No fowl or field mouse that night of his kneeling
Lies in the fox's fires
Or twice dies in the screech-owl's eyes;

All the Canterbury tales in the wild hedge-
Row of the small, brown friars,
The lithe reeve and the rustling wife
Blithe in the tall telling of his pitch
Time go sleeping

Under the switchback glide of his tears,
(And the salt light).
Young Aesop fabling by the coracled Towy

And here the fragmentary poem ends. This is only the first part, left incomplete. There would certainly have been a second part which would have made the poem parallel in structure, though not in pattern, to 'In Country Sleep', and there might have been a third.

Drawing on Dylan Thomas's exposition in the broadcast, but with no manuscript justification at all, I have improvised an extension for completing the first part. Here it is. Only the first three lines belong to Dylan Thomas' composition:

Under the switchback glide of his tears,
(And the salt light).
Young Aesop fabling by the coracled Towy
Sees, dropped from nowhere, talons
Rending, where herons stab for prey.

He mourns rayed feathers branding the fox in flight
Strewing with cockerel phantoms
Farms in death painting the arms of day,
Still in the silence of dew drenched years
Crowing proudly.

He sings of Country Heaven's patience
(Dark with sleet spears)
Building straw's breathing byre for the child newborn
Guarded from shafts of winter,
Storing flowers' light in coombs and streams.

Always through night, where the mountain face appears
In the ground cloth now withered,
Tinder for fire, charred black, blood redeems
The thunderclap of warring nations'
Flash, plumed with scorn.

He mourns Heaven's countrymen in hedgerows
(Light is their shade!)
Who ask what burned star, which of their turning homes,
Which world of magic spinning,
Plunging from glory, self-destroyed,

Whirled by betrayal, is cast from life, unmade,
Blasted from fledged beginning.
The hedgerow rumour: 'Earth!' breathes on the void;
And they hold in their eyes green meadows,
Streams, byres, and coombs.

Vernon Watkins August 30th, 1966

Quite Early One Morning

by Dylan Thomas

'August Bank Holiday. A tune on an ice-cream cornet. A slap of sea and a tickle of sand. A fanfare of sunshades opening. A wince and whinny of bathers dancing into deceptive water. A tuck of dresses. A rolling of trousers. A compromise of paddlers. A sunburn of girls and a lark of boys. A silent hullabaloo of balloons.

'I remember the sea telling lies in a shell held to my ear for a whole harmonious, hollow minute by a small, wet girl in an enormous bathing-suit marked "Corporation Property".

'I remember sharing the last of my moist buns with a boy and a lion. Tawny and savage, with cruel nails and capacious mouth, the little boy tore and devoured. Wild as seed-cake, ferocious as a hearth-rug, the depressed and verminous lion nibbled like a mouse at his half a bun, and hiccupped in the sad dusk of his cage.'

So begins 'Holiday Memory', broadcast by Dylan Thomas in 1946, the fifth of the twenty-two talks and parts of talks collected in this volume. It is a characteristic passage. To say that the style of these talks is inimitable would be a considerable under-statement. Many writers have been able to evoke the pictures of childhood, but none has done so through the particular medium which Dylan Thomas chose. The excitement is conveyed, not through narrative, but through an exact and intuitive use of words. Verlaine used to try his words out by repeating them, rolling them on his tongue and spitting them out, alone in his room. Yeats sometimes used a similar method, and Dylan Thomas certainly did. When he was looking for an adjective in his poetry he would try fifty or a hundred, and reject them all. Even in his prose, which came to him much more easily, he studied with great diligence the effects of words, and his imagination was satisfied only with such word-linkings and juxtapositions as matched a rooted common experience to anarchy and the element of surprise.

Like all great clowns he was sad; but the gaiety and exuberance of this book are positive and indestructible. We are told on the blurb that it was proposed by the author just before he left on what was to be his last journey to New York; and Mr Aneirin Talfan Davies, of the Welsh B.B.C., who has carefully edited the talks, says in his Preface that this collection constitutes with 'Under Milk Wood' all that can be preserved in print of his contribution to the broadcasting medium in this country. It is regrettable that more has not been preserved, for there were many other talks. One wonders what has happened to his dissertation on Abadan, or why the scripts of his two appearances on television, particularly the second, which was printed in 'The Listener', could not have been added to the book. The editor, who does not refer to these omissions, has divided the talks into two parts, the first twelve relating to the poet's experiences in childhood and afterwards, and the last ten relating to writers and to poetry.

It is impossible to close the book without regret, without an infinite sense of loss. Dylan Thomas as a broadcaster was unique. His place in sound radio was equivalent to Chaplin's place in the silent film. The depth and range of these talks is extraordinary, and extraordinary in its depth and subtle variations was the voice which gave them life. When he broadcast he found it necessary to take off his coat, for he used a great deal of invisible gesture. This was his true medium. In television he was magnificent, but physically uneasy, and he wore his coat.

In his poetry Dylan worked with great patience. He believed there was no harder work than the making of poems, and he understood, too, that the sole purpose of that work was to wait upon those accidents which would make the poem magical and permanent. He expressed these beliefs in a discussion with James Stephens, his part of which is the last item of the book. The discussion itself was perhaps the least satisfactory of all the broadcasts. No sympathetic contact was made between the two poets, and all that emerged from their embarrassing proximity was one irreconcilable monologue impinging upon another in a discordant friction. The moral of this was clear: Dylan's imaginative world was a very complete one, and he was at his best when he was left alone.

It is possible to resent interference of another kind,

though this occurs only at the beginning. The first and earliest of these talks, broadcast at the beginning of 1943, was originally called 'Nostalgia for an Ugly Town'; and it ended in a piece of direct statement. The last sentence of the talk, 'The fine, live people, the spirit of Wales itself', did not belong to the original script, but was diplomatically added, there being an unwritten rule that all talks on the Welsh Service should end with 'the spirit of Wales'. At the same time the title was changed to the dull and much less personal 'Reminiscences of Childhood', lest the ugly town which he loved should be offended. It is true that there is no evidence of interference with the script itself, every phrase of which, except the last, rings true; but even such a small concession, which to a writer means really a very big one, would not have been made a few years later. Producers had then become wiser, and Dylan was wiser, too.

Which of these talks is the best? How is it possible to decide? In only one, on Sir Philip Sidney, does Dylan wear for a short time a mask which does not seem to be his own. Even this is full of brilliant things, but there is less spontaneity because one feels that he would not have carried a historical background to Sidney's poetry in his head, unless he had to. Historical data did, to a certain extent, cramp his style, as though he were collaborating. The most dazzling of all the talks is perhaps 'The Festival Exhibition; 1951', and the most moving 'Return Journey'. In 'Return Journey' he used a soft, quick and intimate voice, the exact tone of his natural conversation. This is the most intimate, the most strictly autobiographical of all the talks, and the most Welsh. It describes his return after the war to bombed Swansea, in search of the child he had ceased to be. He tells it, and the script is dramatised for other voices. The journey ends in the park of the 'Hunchback in the Park' poem, Cwmdonkin Park, where he had played as a child. When he was gathering material for this talk he expounded his plan, and he took great trouble to get the exact sequence of shops in the Swansea streets which had been obliterated in the fire-raids of February, 1941.

It was these talks, into which Dylan poured all the echoes and vitality of his extremely sociable life, which made possible his final masterpiece, 'Under Milk Wood'. In one of them, written in 1945 when he was living in New Quay in Cardiganshire, the first seeds of that masterpiece are already apparent. This is the talk from which the book takes its title. The author walks through the small Welsh sea town in the early morning and watches it waking up.

> 'The town was not yet awake. Birds sang in the eaves, bushes, trees, on telegraph wires, rails, fences, spars, and wet masts, not for love or joy, but to keep other birds away. The landlords in feathers disputed the right of even the flying light to perch and descend.'

The characters of 'Under Milk Wood' are foreshadowed:

> 'What big seas of dreams ran in the Captain's sleep? Over what blue-whaled waves did he sail through a rainbow hail of flying fishes to the music of Circe's swinish island? Do not let him be dreaming of dividends and bottled beer and onions.'

And in the closing verses of the talk, where each verse is given to a character, we meet one of them:

> 'Open the curtains, light the fire, what are servants for?
> I am Mrs Ogmore Pritchard and I want another snooze.
> Dust the china, feed the canary, sweep the drawing-room floor;
> And before you let the sun in, mind he wipes his shoes.'

Incidentally it is a pity that the first sentence of this title-talk has a misprint, a full-stop that should not be there, in the very first sentence, and that the first verse of 'The Hunchback in the Park' on p.11 has the same mistake, but the book is carelessly printed, and words like 'attentuated' on page 19 should not have passed the proof reader.

Two of the talks were recorded at the same time, and they are the last of all: the fragment 'Laugharne' which he wrote for a broadcast about the village where he lived for fifteen years and where he is now buried, and the sardonic but prophetic 'A Visit to America'. Both are as witty and original as anything in the book, the first packed with affection, the second seething with a tolerant disgust. He allied merciless penetration to an acute gift of mimicry and self-parody. He loved life. He loved people, and in certain places he loved the way they lived, but in other places it sickened him. 'Laugharne' is the very last thing he wrote for this book. The recording of this was broadcast four days before he died. The first broadcast of

‘A Visit to America’, which was written a good deal earlier, was scheduled for the day which turned out to be the day of the poet’s funeral, so it was postponed until March, 1954.

From his first beginnings, both in poetry and prose, Dylan Thomas had moved from a haunted, confused and symbol-charged shaping-place in the direction of the living voice. Even at twenty-four he had begun to find it, and from that time the natural world engaged his imagination with increasing power. It was no longer artificial symbols, but living people, and dead people, that he cared for. He never, however, lost his preoccupation with words, and it is doubtful whether any writer, cramming his work with life, joy and gaiety, has used words with greater cunning. The writer he most resembles, in his inexhaustible spring of language and ideas, is Dickens, especially in his list of people at the Festival Exhibition in 1951:

‘...people too bored to yawn, long and rich as borzois, who, before they have seen it, have seen better shows in Copenhagen and San Francisco; eccentric people: men with deerstalker caps tied with rope to their lapels, who carry dried nut sandwiches and little containers of yoghurt in hairy green knapsacks labelled ‘glass with care’; fat, flustered women in as many layers of coats as an onion or a cab-driver, hunting in a fever through fifty fluffed pockets to find a lost packet of bird-seed they are going to give to the parrots who are not there...’

How differently he worked in verse may be seen from his reading and introduction of ‘Three Poems’, in the second section of the book. There, in discussing the ‘poem in preparation' which was to be called 'In Country Heaven', he gives a glimpse of the intensity of that vision, and the strictness of that restraint, which made his poetry so severe a discipline. The poetry was made by isolation, the prose by his social life; yet they acted upon each other, and out of this conflict came a new and miraculous use of language, an exuberant, living language, of which this book is the latest example.

Behind The Fabulous Curtain

Dylan Thomas: The Legend and the Poet, *ed. By E. W. Tedlock. Heinemann. 25 s.*

It is difficult to explain to anyone who did not know Dylan Thomas why any study of him must remain totally inadequate. It is equally difficult to explain why those who knew him find themselves deeply handicapped in writing about him. The quality he prized most was seriousness, and he was a born clown; but was there any other poet of recent times who could create so quickly an intimacy of judgment, an apprehension of what was valid, in art and life? That is perhaps one of the reasons why strangers who met him only once for a long conversation felt, after his death, that they had known him all their lives. The entertainer and the intellectual alike were slightly ashamed after meeting him, as he could beat them both at their own game; but if they were humble they quickly recognised that he was humble, too. The prig was his bête noire, the pedant a black-and-white crossword figure whom he didn't despise.

The variety of life and its abundance sang in his veins. He was born to praise it, and he did so most completely when war distorted it into every manifestation of horror. When the war ended, his own war continued. He was, on the one hand, enriched by the heroic comedy of people's lives, for he loved people, and, on the other, fascinated by artificial pattern, for the problems of form he had to solve in his last poems were subtler and more intricate than any he had set himself before. He found freedom in the late broadcast scripts, but pattern obsessed him. This late work of prose, with all its humorous invention, was made by his social life, the poetry by his isolation in spite of that, the isolation of the entertainer who has taken off his mask.

A writer's mask can be fatal to him, and it is certain that the image the age demanded of Dylan Thomas was accelerated by his popularity. His infectious humour deceived everyone but himself. His method was not to retreat from the mask, but to advance beyond it, and in that exaggeration remain completely himself. He agreed readily with his detractors, and did not at all mind being misunderstood. Then, in the private dark, his exuberance was subjected to the strictest control. The public figure and the lyric poet whose work began and ended in the Garden of Eden came to terms, terms which no critic or friend has the complete equipment to analyze.

EXEGESIS

So many voices
Instead of one.
Light, that is the driving force
Of song alone:
Give me this or darkness,
The man of his bone.

None shall replace him,
Only falsify
Light broken into colours,
The altered sky.
Hold back the bridle,
Or the truth will lie.

The Wales Dylan Thomas Knew

One of the reactions to Dylan Thomas's play for voices 'Under Milk Wood' took an unexpected form. It was, I think, a group in Finland which proposed that missionaries should be sent to Wales to rescue its towns and villages from confusion and primitive horror. This would have delighted the poet even more than the praise which acclaimed his work. What tasks those missionaries would have to face! Dylan loved Wales, and he loved particularly Swansea, where he was born and wrote more than half his poems, and Laugharne, where his finest work in poetry and prose was finished, and where he lies buried.

The basis of Dylan Thomas's work, in all its violent, teeming, comic, tragic, and exuberant imagination, is to be found in Swansea. From his parents' house at the top of Cwmdonkin Drive he projected his carefully constructed early poems over the roofs of the town; and Cwmdonkin Park, with its reservoir which has since been drained, was, in his own words, 'a world within the world of the sea town; quite near where I lived, so near that on summer evenings I could listen, in my bed, to the voices of other children playing ball on the sloping, paper-littered bank; the park was full of terrors and treasures.'

The sea town, the park, and the Gower peninsula stretching from Mumbles to Rhossili, and from Rhossili out to Worm's Head where he was once cut off by the tide for seven hours, supplied Dylan's imagination with all that it needed for the early poetry and prose, and for the collection of stories, begun at the outbreak of war, which for the first time in his work brought to the public in 'Portrait of the Artist as a Young Dog' the rich comedy and evocative brilliance of his conversation. These sprang from his surroundings, sudden or long friendships, stories and acquaintances in the pub, all the contradictory elements of his social life, as his poems, which were his deepest and slowest work, sprang from isolation, when every comic mask had been laid aside. It was, at the beginning of his life and at the very end, the Garden of Eden which he saw, and in all the time between it was Deaths and Entrances which occupied him. 'That is all I have ever written about or wanted to write about,' he told me when he had just begun the poem of that name in 1940, 'and it will be the title of my next book of poems.' Five years were to pass before that book was published.

It is true that Dylan Thomas wrote a certain amount in England: a little in Hampshire at Blashford, a little in John Davenport's house at Chippenham, a little in Oxford, and even a little in London, where he found the conditions for writing most difficult; but it was to Wales that he always returned. Many great writers have only managed to write about their own country, and to interpret it, in exile; but Dylan, away from Wales, always felt his exile a hindrance. In the hut at Laugharne near the Boat House, which was his third and last home there, he found perfect conditions for working at those seven poems of his last seven years which constitute an unfinished masterpiece. Beneath him was the estuary, above him Laugharne Castle, and westward across the water which lapped the wall of the Boat House, was Sir John's Hill. Here,

In my seashaken house
On a breakneck of rocks

he wrote, slowly and patiently, his greatest poetry. Only three parts of his projected poem 'In Country Heaven' were finished, but these are equal to anything he achieved, and the landscape of what is, perhaps, the finest of the three, 'Over Sir John's Hill', is Laugharne.

Dylan Thomas's allegiance to Laugharne lasted from the moment he arrived there, soon after his marriage. On his arrival he wrote to Robert Herring, the Editor of 'Life and Letters': 'Its literary values are firmly established. Richard Hughes lives in a castle at the top of the hill; I live in a shed at the bottom.'

Many of the poems and stories, as well as the radio scripts, draw their imagery, and characters, from Swansea or Laugharne, the two focal points of his work; but 'Under Milk Wood' is a synthesis of two places. Just before his thirtieth birthday, celebrated in the beautiful poem which holds together the two halves of his childhood, 'a child's forgotten mornings' and Laugharne's 'heron-priested shore', he moved with his family to New Quay, in

Cardiganshire, where he wrote the first notes towards a play to be called 'The Town That was Mad'. In New Quay he also wrote the radio script 'Quite Early One Morning', in which a few of the characters of 'Under Milk Wood' already appear. Seven years later, back in Laugharne, he finished and published in 'Botteghe Oscure' the first half of the play for voices under the provisional title 'Llareggub'; but the next year saw many changes, and he was to continue to revise it until the very week of his death in New York.

The only play for voices which Dylan did complete, unalterably, was 'Return Journey', a masterpiece in its own right. This was broadcast in 1947. In it he describes his return to Wales after the war in search of the boy he had been, and the search leads him to Swansea, flattened by bombs, where he arrives and stands among the ruins of buildings he had known, on a February day of falling snow. After exploring the streets and the sands of Swansea Bay, he returns to the Grammar School where he had edited its magazine, and hears the names of those killed in the war who had been pupils there; and finally he retraces his steps to Cwmdonkin Park and speaks to the keeper, who rings his bell as the park closes.

All Dylan Thomas's works are the product of an innocent vision. His way of looking at the world was to see it as freshly created, its creatures as the first of their kind. His reperception of childhood was easy for him, for he had never really abandoned it; in a certain sense he had never left Swansea. As he said in a poem,

> The ball I threw while playing in the park
> Has not yet reached the ground.

It was less easy for him to come to terms with conventional money-making, with what he called, in a letter to me, 'the bowler-treed paths'. So he naturally turned to fantasy for relief, and in Laugharne he found it. London had had its moment of fantasy in the Festival Exhibition of 1951, and this is how Dylan would have wished London to remain. But Laugharne was fantastic always. On November 5th, 1953, four days before his death, his recorded voice came over the wireless, talking about Laugharne to Laugharne itself, and he began:

'Off and on, up and down, high and dry, man and boy, I've been living now for fifteen years, or centuries, in this timeless, beautiful, barmy (both spellings) town, in this far, forgetful, important place of herons, cormorants (known here as billy duckers), castle, churchyard, gulls, ghosts, geese, feuds, scares, scandals, cherry-trees, mysteries, jackdaws in the chimneys, bats in the belfry, skeletons in the cupboards, pubs, mud, cockles, flatfish, curlews, rain, and human, often all too human, beings; and, though still very much a foreigner, I am hardly ever stoned in the streets any more, and can claim to call several of the inhabitants, and a few of the herons, by their Christian names.'

Laugharne is the resting place of the poet:

> 'Six feet deep that name sings in the cold earth'.

But Swansea holds his childhood and his first youth; and the memorial stone in Cwmdonkin Park is inscribed with the last three lines of 'Fern Hill':

‘Oh as I was young and easy in the mercy of his means
   Time held me green and dying
  Though I sang in my chains like the sea.’

Vernon Watkins August 1965

Vernon Watkins On Poetry

Insert for Spectrum

Dr. George Thomas interviewing Vernon Watkins. Transmitted: 16th February, 1967

George Thomas: Well, good evening Vernon Watkins. I'd like first of all to say how very pleased I was to see that the Faber paper-back edition had published a selection of your poetry. I have been looking at the back and you're in very distinguished company – a select group of people who've been selected. I think no one among discriminating readers of poetry will quarrel with the selectors. I'm sure that this in Wales is a very rare and happy situation. Having said that, I must admit that I've known your poetry for over 25 years and I've been trying to ask myself one particular question about this new selection. I trust you will be able to help me to find the answer. How true a picture of your total work, to date, is given by the thirty-three poems? Did you have a definite principle governing your choice of these poems? It must have been very difficult.

Vernon Watkins: It was extraordinarily difficult and I don't select my poetry easily. I'm too attached to the individual poems to see them very clinically and objectively. Well, it was first the question of the number of pages. I found I couldn't contract to sixty pages and Faber's were kind enough to offer me twenty more. Even then I decided that I'd have to leave out all the long ballads which average perhaps one hundred lines or more and, of course, the two longest which are six hundred and seven hundred and fifty lines were quite out of the question. But all the long poems I left out except that I felt that the long poem 'Yeats in Dublin' should go in. For one thing it's been out of print for ten years. It means a great deal to me and of course the poetry of Yeats means a great deal to me.

George Thomas: I'm glad that you've said that you were compelled by conditions of space to have to leave out the ballads. This seems to me a significant kind of poetry that you've written in the past and I wonder if in fact you are very conscious of the need to write poetry that can be read aloud. I was rather surprised in re-reading one of your poems in this selection "The Turning of the Stars' where you say that 'Verse is a part of silence. I have known/ Always that declamation is impure', and I'm wondering if in fact that is a true comment on your use of ballads.

Vernon Watkins: Yes, I think so. I should say first perhaps that I distinguish very much between the ballad form and the lyric. All my poetry is lyrical but the particular part of it which is ballad is different in character because the voices are, as it were, divided. There is more than one voice. A lyric is really the expression of the poet's imagination. But in a ballad individual voices which are anonymous take over – in my ballads at least which are not so much narrative ballads as metaphysical ballads in which two or three people express their feelings and a particular mood, a particular situation. I always aim at getting the ballad as hard and as anonymous as a stone whereas in the lyric I don't want to make the lyric personal. I want to make it true for every person.

George Thomas: You once said that you thought that the ideal state for a poet was to be read by everybody and not be known.

Vernon Watkins: Certainly I feel this. The ideal of the thing is for everybody to love one's poetry and yet to acquire no reputation at all. I think a poet must always move against the flow of his reputation, and always, in a way, disappoint the critics.

George Thomas: Looking back at this selection I noticed with some surprise that the terminal dates of the selected poems are 1930 and 1960. I really came to know your poetry when I was a soldier at the beginning of the last war. Were you, in fact, writing poetry for a very long time before you began to publish? I notice in one of the very arresting poems in this selection, 'The Song of the Good Samaritan', that the singer or speaker of the song says at some point 'Even as a child I began to say 'how far'." Is this a kind of memory of your own early concern with poetry?

Vernon Watkins: Oh yes. I think it was very early – rather like Dylan Thomas who, I think, at seven or eight started writing poetry and was extraordinarily precocious. I also started writing extremely early, without being very precocious. I think my verse remained very derivative until I was nineteen or twenty. But I certainly started when I was about seven. And by the age of nine I was collecting all the English poets I could find as presents to my parents. We had some in the house but I was filling in the gaps. Poetry occupied me continually, right up to the time I went away to school. Then through that time and through Cambridge. Now, at the age of twenty two I had a complete revolution in my imagination and all the poetry I had written really meant nothing to me after that although some of it had been published in a Cambridge Anthology. There was one poem which had got into the London Mercury in 1929. Only, I think, the very light verse that I had done up to that time meant anything more to me really.

George Thomas: Looking over the selection I noticed that some of the poems are quite long and they really stir up the mind. There are two in particular that have stirred me and they're about roots. One is the long poem about Yeats – this is 'Yeats in Dublin' and the other is a poem about Dylan Thomas. I really wanted to ask you something about the Yeats poem first. It seems to me to be a transcript of what Yeats may have said to you but there seems to be a kind of – not a programme for Vernon Watkins as a poet, but Yeats talking about poetry sometimes reads like the way I would like to talk about your own poetry. 'Hard as thoughts in the bone to find / Are naked words to say. Write, get rid of rhetoric/ Cut the dead wood away'. Am I reading far too much into these words of Yeats?

Vernon Watkins: No, I don't think so. The poem is really an account of the actual words he said but in some parts of it I have crystallized a great deal that he said into a more concise form or image. But the history of the poem goes back much further than its date although Yeats himself saw a draft of the poem before it was revised. I wanted to know whether he would object to my reproducing his conversation because had he objected I should not have published the poem. But I had a charming letter from him just as he was leaving for France at the beginning of October 1938, saying 'Please feel free to use any scraps of my conversation in this poem'. He liked the poem.

George Thomas: And there are scraps of his conversation in the poem.

Vernon Watkins: Running through it certainly, yes. Now he died, of course, in January 1939- three or four months after he wrote that letter and on his death bed he was still writing the greatest lines of poetry of his life. It is a very remarkable thing that his poetry always grew and became more fresh as he aged. Well, I've been under the spell of his poetry since 1928 and this is indicated at the beginning of the poem 'After the 10 years silence/ I look him in the eyes'. It was a great experience to meet him and an even greater one to hear him talk. When I left, I went across to Galway with my French friend in the train and he said 'You must write down as much as you can remember of what he said'. So I fished out my writing pad and jotted a lot of notes down. But I didn't look at these notes until nine months later when I finished revising the poem and then I found that I had got most of these things down but in a different order.

George Thomas: So tha, in a sense, this is a true record of Yeats...

Vernon Watkins: It is so true that my great friend Dylan Thomas criticized me for making it so literally true. In a letter to me about it, he did express enthusiasm for the poem. He thought it was a very true poem for me to write. But he said that a poem that is so literally a report can be 'a clot of truths' – that was his own phrase and Dylan was a great critic.

George Thomas: This is why I like the poem to Dylan Thomas. You seem to literally be restoring a picture of Dylan.

Vernon Watkins: Well, I gave it this title because I felt that Dylan was most misrepresented by all the people who wrote about him after his death. I didn't write the poem specifically to correct those books and theses and comments, because, had I just wanted to do that, I'd have written in prose. A prose correction is quite as effective. No, I was completely compelled to write it after resisting the idea of writing a poem about him. And the poem came through very true for me, whatever it is for other people. This is the Dylan Thomas I knew.

George Thomas: The two very powerful moments in it for me – "My immortality, he said, Now matters to my soul Less than the deaths of others" – which seems to be the beginning of the poetry in London and has the authentic movement of the beginning of...

Vernon Watkins: Well, the history of this particular sentence is that I remember very distinctly his saying these words to me in a pub with great intensity.

George Thomas: And the other was 'The man I mourn could honour such with every breath he drew. I never heard him wish to take a life from where it grew'.

Vernon Watkins: This is also completely true, I feel. Dylan said that he wasn't at all a political poet. He went through almost surrealist political changes but he fundamentally didn't want to change anything, really. It's very difficult to talk about this because, of course, there were facets of life which disgusted him a great deal. But fundamentally he wanted each person, as I say in the poem, to be where he is and what he is. He didn't like change.

George Thomas: Yes, there's far too much disgust being ladled over his life at the moment.

Vernon Watkins: Oh certainly. He was a very magnanimous person.

George Thomas: Not only in this selection but in fact in some of your other volumes of poetry, I noticed how you are tending, or perhaps you've always tended, to talk about the long dead or people who are dead but seem to be part of the present. I remember one of your poems in 'Affinities' when you were talking about the demands of the Muse. "Always it is from joy my music comes/ And always it is sorrow keeps it true'. Is this a fundamental attitude that comes over readily into your verse?

Vernon Watkins: Oh, I think so. I believe the truth of those two lines very much indeed. I have been criticised for writing more about dead people than living ones, and of being more aware of them perhaps. Also for writing about dead poets. Well, I have even said hard things about the critics though I believe profound criticism can be a very wonderful thing. I have said I owe a great deal to dead poets and I owe nothing to the critics. But as far as the dead go, I feel them as contemporaries. If I write about say Keats or Shelley or Browning as I have done, I almost feel I know them as well as if they entered the room. I would not write about them otherwise. I think really the whole of the past is a simultaneous experience.

George Thomas: This is a very personal idea that runs widely through your poetry. I was thinking of a quotation from the poem 'Peace in the Welsh Hills' – 'That light is present and that distant time/ Is always here continually redeemed'. I would very much like to hear you read "Peace in the Welsh Hills'.

Vernon Watkins: 'Peace in the Welsh Hills'.

George Thomas: Are you actively engaged in writing poems now?

Vernon Watkins: Yes, I'm always writing verse but I'm very slow at finishing it. But it is a more or less continuous activity. I find it very exacting. I trust very much the demands of the poem.

George Thomas: I'm very glad to hear that in fact you are now teaching students.

Vernon Watkins: I find this very interesting. I can't say how good I am as a teacher. All I can say is that I think I learn a lot from doing it. How much they learn is anybody's guess.

George Thomas: And you're going away to America next fall.

Vernon Watkins: Yes, next September.

George Thomas: To Seattle.

Vernon Watkins: Yes, the University of Washington, Seattle.

George Thomas: Will you then be a professor of creative writing?

Vernon Watkins: No, no, I try to eliminate these words creative writing from whatever is their equivalent of the syllabus. They're very fresh out there. They have very fresh ideas of composition, they're very enthusiastic. If you read your poems, the hall is packed. They're full of memories of Dylan Thomas's readings and this is very wonderful. Poetry is a live thing. What they haven't got, I think, is the academic background particularly of English poetry. I love reading poems aloud and I take these jobs as a kind of pretext for doing what I love to do. All my work is written from the ear and intended for the ear. There are some poets who write much more for the eye than I do. I write everything for the ear.

George Thomas: I think that, in fact, your concern to retain forms although not necessarily traditional forms helps this.

Vernon Watkins: Well, I write in very fixed form on the whole. Where I don't use rhyme I write in fixed metric-nearly always, except in some very light things that I don't publish. But this is simply a thing I find necessary to my imagination. One critic, I believe, said – perhaps it was of my last book- that each new book of Vernon Watkins is more old fashioned than the last. Well, of course I've never cared much about fashion. I think a poet has to think in terms of centuries. It's a critic's business to think in terms of decades and to sort out what is happening. Fundamental truths don't change and I'm a metaphysical poet. I'm entirely concerned with those.

George Thomas: It is a fact that form is part of this conflict. In 'Affinities' you said in your 'Demands of the Muse' – 'It is by conflict that he' – I suppose the Muse – 'knows me, And serves me in my way and not another,' {Note by Vernon Watkins: Dr. George Thomas has misunderstood this. The Muse is speaking in the poem, and the poet is 'he'.}

Vernon Watkins: Well, I feel, for instance that Beethoven's music is an account of difficulties overcome. And in a way all verse is like that. T. S. Eliot spoke of it in the 'Quartets' and it was really entirely through T. S. Eliot who liked my poetry that my work was printed in America at all in book form. And he speaks of the intolerable wrestle in the 'Quartets'. This wonderful poetry of the 'Quartets'.

George Thomas: You said a little earlier that you were a metaphysical poet. I notice that as always there are religious, I was going to say overtones, but that isn't true, – undertones in your poetry.

Vernon Watkins: Yes, I'm fundamentally a religious and metaphysical poet. I'm not a nature poet or a descriptive poet. But of course nature is the great pattern of all one"s images. The truths of nature are really inexhaustible. But what compels one if one is a metaphysical or religious poet is the further truth, you see. The hand measure.

George Thomas: I wonder if I could press you to read, not specifically a religious poem, but a poem that seems to me to have this other truth that you've just been talking about. It's a poem called 'Vine', that's happily included in this collection of poems.

Vernon Watkins: Yes, that is the one short poem that I took from 'Affinities'.

VINE

Deep-rooted vine, delay your fruit
Beyond youth's rashness. I have seen
Rich promise wither to the root
Before its time had been

Drain all the darkness of the soil
And stand there shrivelled, crisp and dry,
Too lifeless in your parchment coil
To open one green eye
Some watch the March winds animate
Those early bulbs in Winter's bed.
Envy them not, but keep your state.
Let others think you dead.
Contain in secrecy that balm
Strengthening the sap before it moves,
That the broad leaves from wells of calm
One day grow dark with love

I know a tree as dry as yours.
The patient leaf is put forth late.
Its life is an anchored in the hours
For which the heart must wait.

Poetry and a Career

This questionnaire has, I believe, been sent to writers of all kinds, but I am only able to answer it from the point of view of a poet.

I do not think for a moment that a poet can, or should, earn enough money to live on by writing only poetry. He would have to act as a window-dresser to his most secret property and parade 'that one talent which is death to hide' instead of guarding it with the reticence which belongs to revelation. Also he would depend upon appreciation, so there would always be a temptation to write in order to please, rather than to satisfy the thirst of his imagination.

Yet a poet must live, and he knows that his life involves two difficulties. The first is the difficulty of his task, for poetry is compounded of revelation and labour: without the revelation the labour of all the analytic and harmonizing resources of ear and intellect the revelation will remain an unspoken thing, a book behind the eyes.

The first process is momentary, but the second, even in a short poem, may involve months or years of struggle. It is the hardest thing to match the moment. The second difficulty involved in a poet's life is his realization that compromise is fatal to poetry. All professional offers must be refused. He will not become rich, except by remaining poor.

A poet, therefore, has to choose. I do not myself think that the choice matters much, but it is always significant. If Dante had been a steeplejack and Milton a deep-sea diver I can still believe that their works would have been written, though not exactly as we have them to-day. What is the choice confronting a young poet to-day? Work is demanded of him in return for the necessities and benefits of living. If he is skilled at any particular work distinct from his writing he is fortunate; otherwise he is left with two alternatives. He can either do cultural work that is related to his own art, or he can choose something else, and begin at the beginning. He understands that the mass of people who are called 'the public' do not on the whole care for poetry or find any use in it. They are called 'Philistines' by men and women of aesthetic sensibilities. They are indifferent. Possibly he has met people whose wrong-headed interest in poetry seemed to him more repugnant than indifference, and is looking for respite. Anything is better than the false. It remains for him to find out exactly how false the so-called 'Philistines' are.

The poet who undertakes cultural work for a living and remains in it always will never be able to tell him, for he will be speaking always of a country he has not entered, except as a spy. The poet who chooses his career in the camp of the 'Philistines', where the ability to write poetry earns him no respect, may also be considered a spy. This may or may not be true – everything depends always on character and the individual – but one thing is certain: if he is a spy, his espionage is of a different kind. The difference lies in the fact that he finds himself in two unknown countries, not one; he must examine his own sensibilities with a new caution, for people are not now as he expected to find them. A casual, perhaps a jeering reference to poetry, to his overwhelming interest, may revive an adolescent dream and almost restore his former position, but he knows at once that it is no longer true, that it bears only a false relationship to living.

The practical consequences of the choice are never predictable. Leisure is more valuable and more creative than employment, but with much leisure the gain in time may become a loss in intensity; and the advantage, for a poet, or possibly the danger, of long periods of leisure, is incalculable. A great lack of leisure is bound to cost him a good deal of reading and learning, if he wanted that, or travel, if he wanted that, or experience of places and people, if he wanted that, or the practice necessary to his craft. If, however, the poet knows at all times that the first need of his consciousness is to witness, and that his native way of witnessing is found only in poetry, he will not mind what obstacle is put in his way to suppress or delay it. For the inevitable part of poetry will always be written. That is why I think a poet can do any work in the world and not lose by it, provided that he is a poet first. Beethoven rejoiced in difficulties because he knew his power to overcome them, and a poet's work is always strengthened, not by outside help, but by that inner conviction.

It has been suggested that the State might help writers by giving them money. On the whole I think this might be a good thing provided that nothing were asked in return. The State can only solve some of the difficulties, such as poverty and homelessness, that may beset the artist; it can do nothing for art itself. The State would give house and garden to an industrious writer, on one condition: that he would not have to write well. Because it is appalling to oppress the imagination I say this. To be told that you write well is bad enough, but to be told that you have to write well is intolerable. For a poet knows that it is just when he feels that he is writing well, and doing only that, that he ought to stop. The functional skill, though necessary, and itself a reflection of inspired faith, he knows to be the least valuable part of his achievement. For a poet does not write for a short lease; he writes for a moment, and for centuries. He is linked with all ages, and all he needs is stillness, attention.

I asked Yeats how a poet should earn his living, and he said, "That is one of the problems of the Future." But I myself feel certain that a condition of employer and employee existing between the State and the poet will never be satisfactory. If possible a poet should always work out his own way and keep his independence; he may, like Browning, live in an Italian palace, or, like Blake, live in poverty and exultation. Blake was also a great designer, a skilled illustrator and engraver, and he made his own books from plates. By the aid of two arts he was just able to keep his wife and himself alive. Nor did luxury spoil Browning, for his love of painters overcame the splendour that surrounded him, and his interest in people, alive and dead, ran counter to his advantages and undermined his palace like the rats of Hamelin. These are successful examples. There are many abject ones. Great wealth and great poverty can embarrass a poet almost equally, and, of the two, wealth is the greater danger. A few francs could make Verlaine richer than all Byron's fortune made him. The State should rescue poets dying of poverty and put them in 'leisure-homes' perhaps, but it should be a last resort. Nothing should be expected of them, but they would be given opportunities to do manual work or learn a craft. I cannot see the State agreeing to such terms. "What," the State Secretary will whine, "do we get out of this?" And he will go on to refer, with logical misunderstanding, to the National Debt.

Vernon Watkins July 1946

For Whom Does a Poet Write?

Before reading a selection of my poems I mean to ask one question only: for whom does a poet write? If I were to expound many autobiographical secrets it would only confuse the issue, for the Muse of Poetry is immovable and demands only one thing of a poet, that he should organize, with the greatest skill possible, the truth revealed to him. If the demands of the Muse are narrow, the poet must work within those limits. He is moving in time while the Muse is timeless, and his own progression can best be discerned when it is entirely sacrificed to the Muse. The activity of a poet is the opposite of persuasion. His steps are very much those of a man under sentence of death. I do not mean that a poet should lose interest in the affairs of the world, or that, through being a poet, he loses access to the deepest joy accessible to man. Quite the contrary. I mean that, whatever his activity, a poet is never free, never released from a bond. It is possible that the bond was created for him by the works of other poets which leave his own desire unfulfilled. One thing alone is certain, that the bond was predetermined, and that it cannot be revoked.

I begin by saying that a poet writes for an audience of one, and that no audience, however wide, will be satisfied unless he first obeys that law. That is, after all is said, the audience of the Book of Job, of Dante's Comedy, of English lyric poetry from Marvell to Yeats and of French from Villon to Verlaine. Yeats was conscious of the necessity of an audience, but all his poetry was beaten out by the conflict of a dialogue within himself the results of which were awaited by a permanent audience for poetry which he estimated at one thousand souls.

In a time of crisis, and especially in our time, should not a poet write for a wider audience, and put himself in the background? Is not the rhetorical manner of exhortation, the manner of Whitman or of Claudel, better suited to our time, so that the needs of mankind, faced with terrible choices, may be met? One is reminded of the words of Wilfred Owen, who said: 'The whole duty of the poet today is to warn'. Those words are as true now as when they were written, but the Muse is as inflexible as ever: the best instrument of warning is the tract, and poetry remains the instrument of harmonious and indestructible truth. A tree is consumed by fire. Even when this has happened it is the duty of the poet to celebrate the leaves.

A poet's words should, I think, compel the attention of those who do not share his belief: to that extent only he may act as a protagonist, unless he commits himself to prose. Yet even then the quarrel should be his own quarrel; the words may be shaped by his belief, or, as in the case of Wilfred Owen, by his distrust, but he remains a man caught up in a dialogue which may then, or a century later, be overheard by the rest of the world, or may not be heard at all. The last alternative should not discourage the poet, the validity of the work is his concern; its discrimination is the concern of others. For him Yeats' counsel is best:

> Be secret and exult,
> Because, of all things known,
> That is most difficult.

I was twenty-two when my poetry underwent its most violent change. Up to that age all my poems, and there must have been a thousand, were written out of an oppressive urgency in conflict with time. After that age I knew that, whatever happened to me, time would have no power over my work. I was against all publication until I was thirty, when Dylan Thomas, whom I had met a year before, persuaded me to send a couple of poems to the new magazine *Wales,* which Keidrych Rhys was to edit. What made me very angry was that he altered one of the poems a little and I had to go into the Swansea bookshop where there was a high stack of copies and alter them all back. Dylan Thomas and I had a deep affinity. We were both Welsh, both religious poets, and our poetic methods were as unlike as possible, he beginning with a ball of phrases which he moulded into a symmetrical shape, and I with a musical cadence, almost out of earshot, to which I slowly gave substance. Although we had a great affinity of theme our work was complementary. Another bond was that we both believed that a good poem was one which could never be fashionable. He was acutely critical, more critical than professional critics might imagine. He once wrote to me that all criticism of a poem which was not reasons for praise was suspicion. Yet he did not want praise or care about it. In public he was invariably modest about his own work, but in private he was sure of it. When I tried to persuade him to keep two obscure poems out of his second book, which came out in 1936, on the grounds that the reviewers would fall upon those two poems rather than on the best, he smiled and replied: 'Give them a bone.'

That was more than twenty years ago. Since then critics have said some serious things and a great many silly ones. One of the silliest was announced two or three years ago by a critic of great repute. He thought that the acclamation of Dylan Thomas's poems was illusory, and that we should wait to see where Dylan Thomas's reputation stood in five years' time. So strange a confusion of thought would have amused Dylan Thomas.

For me lyric poetry which is not exalted is not worth writing. My own poetry is metaphysical. A poem makes very great demands, always of a minute kind and usually stretched over a long period. The demands are recurrent, like a metronome whose interval may be a minute, a month or a year. My experience is that, however long a poem takes, in the end it is the flash of a moment to get it right. The parts of the poem depend on toil, but it is an accident which adjusts the parts to give a poem unity and make it move.

I think a book, too, should have the accidental unity of a poem unless it is a comprehensive retrospective collection, for that would have only the unity of the poet's life. For this reason I kept out of my first three books some of my early sea ballads which appeared in the fourth book, *The Death Bell*, in 1954, sixteen years after two or three of them were written. They belonged to the same pattern as 'The Ballad of Culver's Hole', which was written early in the fifties. A poet must wait; and, as Molière remarked, 'Le temps ne fait rien a l'affaire'.

In lyric poetry there is no competition. In satirical verse or in verse translation there can be, for those depend on a different kind of concentration. A satiric poet or a translator must, even in the act of writing, occupy the position of critic, but a lyric poet cannot occupy that position until his work is done. The best lyric poetry is made, I believe, out of affirmation, and the best satiric poetry out of disgust. It is true that disgust may be absorbed into great lyric poetry, as it is sometimes in Baudelaire or in the last poems of Yeats. Still, the demands of the Muse are exalted demands; and I repeat what I have said before: lyric poetry that is not exalted is not worth writing.

18th May 1957

On the Writing of Poetry

If I were not myself a practitioner, I might feel very differently about writing poetry. In theory I believe in every variety of poetic activity, in every creative form, but in practice I find myself much more compelled by a certain kind of poetry than by other kinds.

I feel that a poet cannot choose his material, that it is offered to him in an uncompromising way. My own experience is that I am always pulled back to the demands of a poem from the wide, speculative areas which lie outside it. As for other poets, I am sure that it is better for a poet to give all his attention to the object of his imagination, even with a total disregard of the issues of our time, than to give a part of it to those issues from a feeling of duty.

Certainly my poetry depends, for its existence at all, on a religious attitude to life.

I believe that lyric poetry is closer to music than to prose, and that it should be read as exactly as a musical score. I also believe that it is always a gift, the reward of tenacity and minutest attention, and that unless it comes out of exaltation or moves towards it, it is not worth writing.

I suppose every writer, in applauding another's work, undergoes a modulation of sensibility, but I cannot see how any poet whose roots are deep can be fundamentally influenced by a living contemporary. I never think a true style can be learnt from contemporaries.

A good poem is one that can never be fashionable. What is fresh must also be ancient, and a good poem is not finished until it attains its most ancient form. The more ancient a poem is, the more modern it becomes; and will remain so, when apparent modernity is obsolete.

The handling of language is inexhaustibly mysterious. To write poems in the order of natural speech can be very good, but that is by no means the only criterion of excellence. Every restrictive theory of writing leads to monotony, and unforgettable poetry springs only when theory is abandoned, and from recognition that the order of imaginative emphasis is right, whether it is the order of natural speech or not. Natural speech is a corrective ofartificial poetic diction, but form is itself artificial, and unless the artificial demands of form are satisfied in a poem, its impulsive life will not be held in a lasting form.

I think every age is as good and bad as possible for writing poetry. The more the fledgling is pampered, the sillier it becomes. There is now an abundance of talent in Britain and America. Some poets employ strict form, others what is almost a prose idiom. The potentialities of prose as a medium of communication must not be underestimated, but ultimately one is bound to ask whether the virtues of the poem are prose virtues. Perhaps, if they are truly memorable, it does not matter.

Vernon Watkins Nov. 1961

The Second Pressure in Poetry

It is the time of year when readers congregate, when ideas cluster round an unseen point in the sky, the season for the migration of anthologies. There are readers who look for a message, or a new kind of syntax; there are those who expect a portent, or a clever synthesis of what they already know. There are those who want to know where they are going, and others who want to stay where they were. Some look only for innovation, and others are armed to the teeth against anything new. It seems that nothing will ever reconcile so many opposites or draw to a single point such varied and contrary dispositions. I am speaking of people who say that poetry matters to them, whether it is past, present or future. Yet they move, and are moved, in a way and for reasons which they do not understand. No anthology will ever be made that will satisfy all of them. If they happen to be poets, no anthology will ever be made that will satisfy even one.

An anthology of contemporary poetry is supposed to

reflect the time, the Zeitgeist, better than the work of a single poet, but its whole interest for a poet is in the single works outside it which it represents; he uses it only as a pointer to those individual poets for whom he deeply cares. Imaginatively it is always more rewarding to read one poet at a time than to read many.

What do I find in a poet's separated work that I do not find in an anthology? I find contradictions, the interplay of light or shadow among all the poems, the mystery of self-renewal or, if the imagination is stubborn, the refusal to change. All these things may become evident in an anthology, but only if the poet's work is separately known.

When I was nine I began to collect the English poets, and for many years I identified poetry as spontaneous genius pouring through the poet and requiring no effort from him. From then until my early twenties I wrote pretty continuously, except for one year at about fifteen, when I stopped. In my teens I distrusted in composition what did not come rapidly, and I looked on revision as an impediment to the stream. I knew that *Adonais* had been written in five days, and I saw inspiration as the source of light, the original brilliance which could only be tarnished by the deliberating mind.

In two things I have remained constant to my first impression of the nature of poetry. I believe, as I did then, that lyric poetry is closer to music than to prose. And I believe in the gifts of instant and unalterable truth which a poet cannot predict, and for whose coming he must wait. I think it extremely rare for these gifts to come as whole poems, but they are the parts of a poem which a poet must never discard, however hard he has to work to find their true place in the composition.

I no longer associate art with the natural man. Metaphysically I have taken sides. I am interested only in work of the second pressure. True spontaneity, true art, seems to me to come, more often than not, long after the poem's first conception; it is the more powerful for being delayed, and the purer for having been tried in the furnace of contraries. The poem cannot live until it has been willing to die; it cannot fly like the phoenix until it has been consumed by its own flames. Everything seems to me shallow that is not related to an inner experience which changed the man. There is nearly always, in any serious poet, a moment of change, a pivotal crisis in time, that renews him.

In modern poetry there is no more conspicuous example of creative self-renewal than Yeats. He never became a cynic, a man who stopped learning, but remained an artist, a man who continued to learn, all his life. A work of art which has wisdom has also innocence to renew itself, and this Yeats knew. He had already repudiated the style of his early work when, in his fifties, he wrote an essay, 'If I were four-and-twenty'. In this essay he remembers that when he was twenty-three or twenty-four a sentence began to form in his head: "Hammer your thoughts into unity", and that for years after that he tested everything he did by that sentence.

The very humility by which an artist recognizes the total insufficiency of what he has done may be a means of renewal, and to this Yeats gives sacred and arrogant expression in the poem 'To a Friend whose Work has Come to Nothing', where he speaks to Lady Gregory about her work in terms of his own experience:

Now all the truth is out,
Be secret, and take defeat
From any brazen throat,
For how can you compete,
Being honour bred, with one
Who, were it proved he lies,
Were neither shamed in his own
Nor in his neighbours' eyes?
Bred to a harder thing
Than triumph, turn away
And like a laughing string
Whereon mad fingers play
Amid a place of stone,
Be secret and exult,
Because of all things known
That is most difficult.

That is a poem written in the bare, strong style of Yeats' later verse. The style itself is the reward of great conflict, a struggle with an earlier, ornate style which he had used in his first poetry and which had found many imitators. It is a poem of the risen phoenix.

It had taken Yeats a long time to match his own renewal in his style, for stubbornness is another characteristic of the genuine artist. In spite of the experience which anticipates a change of style, a writer who has used the first style with intensity is reluctant to change it. It is even a mark of integrity not to change until the integrity of the new style is established. Who would leave the known field he loves for the unknown field the imagination has shown him in a flash of lightning? Yet the moment of change, the moment of renewal, is unmistakeable when it comes, and after that it is only a question of time.

In the case of Yeats it probably took twenty years for his style to catch up with the experience of his imagination, and that is not an unusual time-lag for a great poet. When I met him six months before he died, with a lifetime of poetry behind him, he was occupied with renewal, with the miraculous element which makes a poem. He had already described his late poems, when he was old and infirm, as 'moving continually, like Swedenborg's angels, towards the dayspring of their youth.' And now he talked about the difficulty of getting rid of poetic diction. 'One is always cutting away the dead wood,' he said. And he told me about an old man he had met in America who had said to him: 'There will always be miracle, there will always be revelation.'

Theory and Act

No permanent good in poetry can come from a restrictive theory of writing. The poet, or group of poets, equipped with such a theory, may issue a manifesto which will signpost a way of writing verse for a generation, and this will always prove a convenience to critics concerned with the prevailing movement of a time. The perceptive critic must be on his guard, and his task is really to distinguish between theory and act. However intelligent a poet's theory may be, it does not bear fruit until the intervention of the creative act; the poem itself masquerades as its offspring, a kind of sandwichman bearing the advertising boards. A true analysis of the poem will nearly always be in conflict with the theory it carries, for the struggle of a theory is one thing and the struggle of a poem another. The value of a theory lies only in its power to attack and purge, but the value of a poem issues from terms of peace. So far as the poem is concerned, the sandwichman is advertising a campaign that is over.

How can one be sure that human judgement is a less solid thing than the act of a poem? Why should a poem, whose origins are so elusive, be necessarily more valid than the critical judgement assessing it or the critical theory which precedes it?

This I can only answer by example. An unresolved poem seems to me to be tendentious in the way in which theory is tendentious, but a resolved poem or play in verse is no longer theory. *Hamlet*, or *King Lear*, no longer advertises any theory of writing, because more has been added in the course of composition than human judgement could reasonably have presupposed. The general syntax of a poem or play may be governed by theory, but its essence, or 'act', as I have called it, is conditioned by the whole imagination, and by something, a kind of luck, which theory could not predict, so that it overleaps the bounds of any restrictive category. I hope that I do not undervalue human judgement, but I feel that it is extended, or delivered from its limitations, by such works.

The tendentious in verse reflects the tendentious in thought, and so belongs to theory rather than to act. Poetry affirms, or it does not exist. The affirmation may be subtle rather than bold; it may be at pains to avoid what Verlaine in his *Art Poétique* called 'la Pointe assassine' in favour of the nuances which he advocated, but affirmation it remains, and particularly affirmation through cadence. The recognition that in a sense all art is fragmentary and can only be completed by love is itself affirmation of the deepest kind. That is why certain lines of poetry, not in themselves dogmatic, are so compelling.

It is the tension between belief and form that gives

intensity to a work of art, just as it is the intervention of luck that gives permanence. In a perfectly resolved poem form and belief are so closely identified that they are indistinguishable: the form is the meaning. This does not necessarily involve the statement of dogma. A poet may or may not hold a fixed, dogmatic belief: if he does, he may still keep it out of his poetry; if he does not, he may yet use it in his art. I am merely saying that the compulsion of a poem involves belief; if it lacks or ignores belief, it is bound to remain a superficial exercise, of no interest to the reader except as a display of skill.

Poets in whom belief strongly predominates over theory will always leave a characteristic imprint on everything they touch, and will more strenuously than speculative poets handle the demands of form. Without a bridle there is no grace, without restraint no strength, without strictness no freedom. The strictest verse in French poetry is Villon's and it is at once the sparest and the most exuberant. Every avenue of expression is open to him because he has chosen a narrow road. Intensity of belief, far from restricting a poet, gives him range. A metaphysical poet, whether he be Donne or Blake or Yeats, cannot write without being involved in belief, and his belief is tested by every contact with life, and renewed every day. Without a compass there is no voyage. The needle trembles, but it returns to the same point.

Poetry and Experience

It is very much easier to talk about another person's poetry than about one's own. I do not mean that one has not a lot to say about one's own, but that one is not able to see, as one does with another poet, the mask that is presented to the world. The finished work obeys certain principles of form derived from tradition; these may be qualified or violated by the particular idiom of the poet, who receives his material from tradition, tests it upon his pulse, and then hands it back with the imprint of his experience. One work follows another, and a *persona* is created, a manner of handling form peculiar to the poet becomes discernable. We say, 'This is a typical poem by Hardy' precisely because Hardy has created this persona which becomes attachable to a certain manner of writing. I am very doubtful, however, whether Hardy himself would have understood the words at all. He would not have been able to see his work from the outside, nor to define its boundaries. Unless it was a direct parody, such as John Betjeman has produced, any trespassing upon the ground of Hardy's *persona* would be apparent to everyone else before it was understood by Hardy himself.

A poet, then, is not, or should not be, handicapped by what is expected of him. The more intensely he works, the less likely he is to burlesque his own style. Yet his work is bound to have, in the end, a unity which an obstinate integrity alone could give it and which no amount of critical perception could foresee. One reason for this is that although, when a part of the finished work is published, the materials for the critical judgement are made available, the labyrinth in which he works remains inaccessible. The craftsmanship may be examined, but all the rewards of craftsmanship defy analysis. Those very elements which make a poem permanent were received by the poet unexpectedly, he is only responsible for them insofar as his toil and persistence prepared for their possibility and left him unsatisfied until the lightning moment of co-ordination.

When I go over the drafts of a poem why do I find them all unsatisfactory? They represent an incomplete experience. In some I see those valid elements which belong to the poem, in others ingenuities of language, thought good at the time of composition, which turn out to be obstructions, impurities which belong to the sophistication of time. All revision is towards an instant thing. The more ancient a poem is, the more modern it becomes; and a lyric poet triumphs only when he gives his poem its most ancient, and therefore most durable, expression. By ancient I do not mean archaic: I mean the freshest and hardest language possible, so handled that its impact is of an ancient kind. The Muse of poetry is timeless, but a poet lives in time. His work is only complete if he observes two fidelities, one to his own experience and his own time, the other to the timeless and heroic truths with which he feels an imperceptible bond.

I have been lucky enough to write two poems in the same evening, only one line of which, belonging to the first poem, I wanted later to change; but it is a commoner experience with me for a year to go by before I finally get right what I first drafted. I blame this partly on my own clumsiness. Facility itself breeds error which only persistence will purge away. There is a tremendous second pressure in poetry. True spontaneity in the poetry I cherish is always of this kind, a purgation and a corrective: only when the soul casts out the impurities of the poem and burns them, can the phoenix of the final and valid poem rise from the flames.

I began writing poetry when I was eight or nine years old, and I began collecting the English poets at ten. Within two years I must have bought twenty of the great poets, but there was nothing really precocious about this. It was not until thirty years later that I understood the plot of 'Maud'. I was dominated by each poet in turn, and my ambition was so shallow that I usually identified the longest poem as the greatest; and at my preparatory school I counted every night the lines of the Arthurian epic I was writing. When I went on to my public school I stopped writing for eighteen months, but then a lecture on Shelley by one of the masters brought back the irresistible impulse, and I wrote poems again, or else they occupied me, fairly continuously. By this time, too, the number of pages in a poem ceased to magnetize me, and a single poet was likely to hold office in my imagination much longer – as long, perhaps, as an American President. Gradually I understood that a poet whom I had read almost exclusively for a year could not be deposed with ignominy and executed; his hold on my imagination was much stronger than I had supposed. At the age of twenty-one the poems and letters of Keats, and the poetry of Shelley, Milton and Blake so governed me that the everyday world hardly existed for me except as a touchstone for protest and indignation. My poems of this time, which were long and continuous, were completely overshadowed by their styles, or else moved in a direction which I afterwards found to be false.

I had begun to see in Yeats the example of a poet whose integrity and sincerity deepened with age. No lyric poetry of our time gave me such excitement, for Yeats taught me, as no other poet had done, how a poet should grow old, without losing any of his freshness or intensity of vision. I was absorbed in Blake's Prophetic Books, but those tremendous visions which Yeats had studied in all their detail lacked personal statement, and this appeared in the new poems of Yeats with piercing clarity.

In my twenty-third year I suddenly experienced a complete revolution of sensibility. I repudiated the verse I had written and knew that I could never again write a poem which would be dominated by time. It took several years for my style to catch up with this experience, so powerful were the verbal legacies left me by the poets I had admired for so long. I now saw them in a new light, but I could not translate my transfigured vision of the world into language. In 1933 I was already making versions of two poems for my first book, 'After Sunset' and 'Thames Forest', and two years later, when I met

Dylan Thomas, those poems were still incomplete. He did see both poems in early drafts on the very first day I met him, for he came to my house and asked to see 'any poems I had.' When he had seen two or three, he asked if there were any more, and I dragged in a trunk from the next room.

Dylan Thomas quickly showed me what was fresh in my work, and what was stale and derived from other poets, not really belonging to myself. We had immediately a very deep affinity, though his style and method of composition were completely different from mine, he working outward from a colloquial core of texture, I working towards the concrete from a musical or articulated source. Although he was much shrewder than I was, our work was, and is, in fact complementary.

I had set myself against publishing, and against sending poems away to a magazine; and Dylan Thomas had set himself against giving titles to his poems. He gave them numbers, like musical compositions. We reformed each other. I persuaded him to use titles; and when the magazine 'Wales' was launched by Keidrych Rhys in 1937, in spite of my hesitation, he picked up two of my poems, altered one of them, and sent them in for the first number. I altered back every copy I could find in Swansea, but the damage was done. A contact was made, and my reticence was broken. I was glad to find that it did not affect composition at all.

The two poems in the first number of 'Wales', 'Griefs of the Sea' and 'Old Triton Time', were among those which I collected for my first book in October, 1940, and which Faber and Faber published a year later. The title was 'Ballad of the Mari Lwyd & Other Poems'. T. S. Eliot was uneasy about the title because he thought that in England and Scotland people would mistake it for a book about Marie Lloyd. 'She deserves such a tribute,' he wrote, 'but in this case it would be misleading.' After many alternative suggestions which held up the book, the original title was accepted, and I had a further note from Eliot saying that he hoped it would not grieve me to return to my first love. It did not.

I suppose every poem in the book rests upon the paradox of life being given back in imperishable terms after it had been logically surrendered to time and death. This is my particular country, my raison d'être, if you like, but it would be unfair to expect a critic to arrive at so simple a definition. I have an exact verbal memory, and my memory of people is not a transient one; so, when the accident of death removed certain people and cancelled the words they said, I could not forget them. Hardy, whose compassion for people was great and whose understanding of character was acute, used these two things in some of his most evocative and beautiful poems. His characters rest in their graves in the faded colours of their existence, and there is infinite pathos in his vivid recollection of them. Such poems are dominated by death's finality and the supersession of time; it is now only the poet's memory which gives these people life. There could be no greater contrast than this to my own belief. Man is spirit; spirit is indestructible; the grave is equally a place of rest and a runner's mark for inconceivable energy, a place where the centuries will be outlived and made obsolete by instantaneous judgement.

In my long 'Ballad of the Mari Lwyd', which means in English 'Ballad of the Grey Mare', I have attempted to bring dead and living together, on the last night of the year, when the skull of a mare, or else a wooden model of a horse's head, was traditionally carried from house to house in Wales by a party of wits and singers demanding food and drink, which they would earn only by succeeding in a rhyming contest with those inside the door. The dead come to the window, and I make them three times as human and cunning and violent as the living. I also show their terrifying thirst, their need of the living, whom they accuse of a total lack of compassion. I cannot read all six hundred lines, but here is a part:

THIRD FIGURE: Bones of the dead should come on their knees

...

Midnight. Midnight. Midnight. Midnight.
Hark at the hands of the clock.

The Ballad had been suggested to me on the last night of 1938 by a broadcast of the ritual of Mari Lwyd from my father's old home in the village of Taff's Well, near Cardiff. I had been working late in Swansea that night, and when I arrived home at a quarter-to-twelve the broadcast was already on. I had a distinct vision, such as one sometimes has when one is tired; and in the next four months I worked at the ballad almost every night. I kept nothing of those hundred pages except the stanza form, and only after another two months did the first verse of the final ballad come to me. The whole poem came, with the refrains, in the following winter.

Some poems from the book are more closely related than the Ballad to the particular time at which I wrote them, and one is the Elegy I wrote for the American film-actress Pearl White, the heroine of the silent film serials which I used to watch with terror every Saturday afternoon at the Uplands Cinema in Swansea at the age of eight or nine. In those days outside the cinema there was a brass railing which seemed to have been designed to keep the Saturday mob of children at bay, and over this we swarmed, at two o'clock, when the doors opened. Our excitement was great. Not for a week had there been any hope for the hero and heroine of our film. On the previous Saturday he and Pearl White had fallen into the trap of the masked villain, deaf to our united cries, and had been finally shown, as the words TO BE CONTINUED NEXT WEEK flashed on the screen, in a situation which offered no solution but death. When we all rushed in, a majority audience of children, some of whom were regularly thrown out, even in the uproar I could not for a moment forget Pearl White, the American actress who really threw herself off bridges into rivers and risked her life in the making of the film. It was war-time, and in our mock street-wars she became the centre of many fights and struggles.

I grew up out of her memory. Then, one day more than twenty years later, in 1938, when the danger of a new war was coming nearer, I suddenly saw on a newspaper poster the four words PEARL WHITE IS DEAD, and this prompted, soon afterwards, the poem which I had always owed her:

> Who flung this world? What gangs proclaimed a truce,
> ...
> Through your three hundred deaths, now Death wears black.

Almost immediately after the publication of this first book of poems I left Swansea for the R.A.F. At my first two stations I was prevented from writing by the impossibility of finding anywhere to sit down, but when I was posted to Calshot as a policeman, one of my duties was to collect and arrest the drunks off the last train. This gave me an opportunity to read in the station waiting-room while they tottered home to bed, and I used to follow them half an hour later without causing them any inconvenience. I usually did twelve hours' night duty, but then I had twenty-four hours off, sometimes even longer, and I cycled regularly to Beaulieu, where I could write and have tea in a walled garden. Later, at Bletchley, I had still more opportunity to do my own work. I continued my poem 'The Broken Sea', the longest of the three poems in my second book, 'The Lamp and the Veil', published at the end of 1945, the other two poems being 'Sea-Music For My Sister Travelling' and 'Yeats In Dublin', an account of my meeting Yeats there and of what he said in July, 1938. I also drafted translations of Heine's 'North Sea' poems in my R.A.F. hut, and these were later printed in a hand-set American book which was reprinted here in 1955.

Meanwhile, early in 1946, I had been demobilised and was back in Swansea. I had written many short poems during the war as well as before and after it, and in 1948 I collected about fifty of these and called the book 'The Lady with the Unicorn', named after the last poem I had composed, on the famous tapestry which I had seen in Paris. This book has, like the first, elegiac poems, poems prompted by the immediate and the concrete, but celebrating the miraculous poise of life between light and darkness. It opens with one which was suggested in winter by a fall of snow on the sea cliff where I live. I walked out on the cliff and found that the foam of the sea, which had been brilliantly white the previous day, now looked grey. This poem is called

'Music of Colours – White Blossom'
Transfiguring whiteness into shadows gone,
... Utterly secret. I know you, black swan.

In another poem of the book, 'Foal' I speak of the gathered thread of which there is no recollection, of the invisible support of the dead. The race of the newborn foal is itself a re-creation of the light of a buried world;

'Foal'
Darkness is not dark, nor sunlight the light of the sun
... But a double journey of insistent silver hooves.

Another poem in 'The Lady With The Unicorn' is called 'Arakhova and the Daemon'. It was written for David Cochrane, an Oxford undergraduate and a son of one of the King's Heralds, to commemorate his death seventeen years before, when he was killed on the slope of Mount Parnassus. Although he was slightly deformed by infantile paralysis, his mind was brilliant, and he struck me as the most original boy at my school. I was reminded of his death when my sister visited the village of Arakhova, near Delphi, a couple of years after the war, and saw the memorial to him cut in stone. In this poem the word Daemon means the soul of the dead:

ARAKHOVA AND THE DAEMON

for David Cochrane, killed on Parnassus 1929

His daemon so transforms that rock,
... That the rough world, not he is is dead.

The title poem of 'The Lady With The Unicorn' was finished on the very evening of the birth of my first son. This prompted me to collect the lyrics of the previous ten years which seemed to form a single pattern. The inexhaustible theme of the book was continued in my next book, 'The Death Bell, Poems and Ballads' which followed in the Spring 1954. A division is made, however, between the long title-poem, the twenty lyrics, and the eight ballads, chiefly about the sea. A ballad writes itself, and, although it is not finished until it is as hard and anonymous as a pebble, or as hard and inscrutable as a shell, it carries the author's voice and his imagination into its own anonymous world. My ballads have much more in common with those of tradition, but they are more concerned with symbols and states of mind than with narrative. The earliest of the ballads, for instance, 'Ballad of the Rough Sea', shows fishermen in danger of drowning, and they have two witnesses, a dead witness who emerges from the middle of the chalk cliff, and a living witness standing on the cliff-top, who are both, perhaps, projections of their own fear. They refuse to be magnetized by the beckoning white finger of the dead man or the treacherous man on the cliff who seems to have arrived casually but is really suspected by them to be a hangman refusing the rope of rescue and intent upon their death:

BALLAD OF THE ROUGH SEA

I like the smell of the wind, the sniff,
... Said a man on the top of Dover cliff.'

Other ballads have their scenery on the Gower Coast, where I live, and so, too, do some of the lyrics in the book, 'The Heron', for instance, which lives on the stream running out into Three Cliffs Bay:

The cloud-backed heron will not move:
...

Constancy within change is the theme of so many of my poems, and until it enters a poem I can never find my imagination wholly engaged. I marvel at the beauty of landscape, but I never think of it as a theme for poetry until I read metaphysical symbols behind what I see. The very wildness of nature and indifference of the sea are the whetstone of the hawk's wing and of the edge of intuitive wisdom which is able to give them grace in another dimension. In a poem for my son, 'A Prayer', I seek the fixed point of metaphysical, unchanging truth, in the turbulence of the waters:

A PRAYER

If I dare pray for one
Gift in the coming age
That might protect my son...

This theme of religious fidelity is again taken up in my most recent book 'Cypress and Acacia', published in

1959, where the poems are almost equally divided between elegiac poems and poems about birth and the expectation of life. Here is a poem of eight lines,

RUTH'S LAMENT FOR NAOMI

I watch the waters glide away
And guard the image they forget.

In my own experience I think of my old landlord, who was for thirty years a musician until he retired to do market-gardening and potter about the field next to my house until his health broke down. He was an extremely independent man, trusting only himself to do the repairs to his own wooden bungalow, which at last he was unable to do. Suddenly one night just before Christmas I found him there sitting in pitch darkness at the point of death. He was rushed to hospital where he died within an hour. While we waited for the ambulance he fainted and knocked out the oil lamp.

He had refused electricity- but recovered and was perfectly sensible when it arrived. This poem is called

A MAN WITH A FIELD

If I close my eyes I can see a man with a load of hay

Another lyric poem, in an equally long line, but almost unrhymed, is 'The Mare'. This is not an elegiac poem but a poem about birth:

THE MARE

The mare lies down in the grass where the nest of the skylark is hidden.

That is an early Summer poem. Here, in Sapphics, is a poem of late Autumn:

GREAT NIGHTS RETURNING

Great nights returning, midnight's constellations
Gather from groundfrost that unnatural brilliance

...

I believe in every variety of music, in every created form. I believe, that is to say, in verse which follows the order of natural speech, and in verse which breaks up that order to impose an order of imaginative emphasis. Both kinds are finally tested by the test of unity: is it, unchangeably and unforgettably, what it is? People have argued strongly against the syntax of 'Paradise Lost', but if it were written in modern idiom it would be a lesser poem. On the other hand, to use the idiom of 'Paradise Lost' is a bad thing, unless you are Milton. One of the characteristics of a true poet is to make theories look ridiculous by imposing his own imaginative order.

Here is a little poem in which I have put down, in couplets, some things which hold true for me in the relationship between poets and criticism. It is published in my latest book of the same title:

AFFINITIES

I find them in the wings of every age
While fools and rhetoricians hold the stage.

I may be wrong, but I believe, as I told Dylan Thomas, that a good poem is one which can never be fashionable.

A true style is never learnt from contemporaries, but always from an affinity with ancient or dead poets. Eliot and Pound, whose names are associated with the revolution in the language of poetry which influences everyone, or nearly everyone, to-day, created that revolution by the study of poets before them, in Pound's case the ancient poetry of China, Provence and Italy, and in Eliot's the French symbolist poets of the nineteenth century and the English dramatic and metaphysical poetry of the seventeenth. They did not, except through such affinities, influence each other.

One recognizes in a poet ancient truths which have been assimilated and re-stated in contemporary terms. Yet a poet's growth is bound to be crooked because he is caught up and corrected at every moment by the intuitive life of his own experience. The response to the Past and the thrust of the Present act upon each other so intricately that the moment cannot be foreseen when the two are reconciled and bewilderment gives place to order. That is why it seems to me that all generalisations about the present state of poetry and its future direction are meaningless. Yeats, and Blake before him, distinguished between the straight line of reason and the crooked line of intuition; both are necessary to each other, but lyrical poetry owes its life to the second. The one is a struggle, the other is a gift.

I am always arriving at different interpretations of what poetry is, and of its relation to experience. All life is lived forward in time, and it sometimes seems to me that a poet is a person who has been made aware of the timeless, and recurrently recognizes it at unexpected moments. Then I remember that to strain towards the timeless is a mistake, as the timeless is already here. It is no good unburdening oneself of the pressure of emotion until the refraction of art has occurred. A poet must wait for art to make possible a true equivalent of life. He must wait until he wants only to unburden himself of the poem. A poem will never happen unless it has first been conceived as a poem. And a true poem, a lucky poem, creates the illusion, if it is an illusion, that it always existed, and that it was waiting only for the poet to write it down.

Vernon Watkins Oct. 1961

Problems of Communication

I am concerned with the links between poetry, music and the visual arts. A poem, a piece of music, a carving or a painting, when it makes a profound impression on the imagination, takes possession, not only of the senses, but of the unconscious mind. The poem, for example, may have an obsessive power for days, causing itself to be repeated over and over again, always with inexhaustible effect. This will go on until the conscious mind is occupied with other things. Even then, the unconscious mind retains it and will bring it to the surface at intervals in the future. In a work of music, melody has the same effect, and the recurrent power of melody returns at unpredictable moments, possessing the imagination. An accident of circumstance or of natural surroundings, an association of landscape with a poet perhaps, may bring a line of verse to mind, but the recurrence of melody seems to obey an almost precise mathematical law, like the expanding ripples from a stone flung in a pool. The exterior world interferes with that law, as wind might interfere with those ripples, but only slightly. Their operation is from the interior world of the imagination, from the stone it has dropped. Such is the aural power of art.

In the visual arts, although there must be the same precision in the unconscious mind, there is not the same exactness of reperception away from the work. A painting alters, however slightly, in the memory; a masterpiece alters; and the sight of it after a lapse of time combines the shock of recognition with an adjustment of the disturbing secret of its power. There is challenge and counter-challenge in its contemplation.

If we turn from the effect of a work of art to its genesis we find a paradoxical situation. The imagination is solitary, and yet, in its potential, holds the attention of millions. It is remembering and expectant at once, as it waits on the unpredictable. The artist is solitary but the need of communication does exist, even for the most solitary of artists. So Milton, when he was overtaken by blindness, spoke of 'that one talent which is death to hide.' A poet does not only address a living audience; equally he addresses the dead and the unborn. When Blake found that nobody would publish his works he was not dismayed. He said that those works were the constant study of archangels, that they were 'published elsewhere', and beautifully bound.'

Just as the artist needs his art to complete his life, so, too, he needs an audience or witness to hear and see it. By giving definition to thought and feeling, he demands a response: once the work is finished, the need of communication exists.

A work will not wholly communicate itself unless the need of communication is banished. If the attention of the artist is intercepted by that need, the work will be incomplete. The position, then, is this: an artist is aware of the need to communicate, and aware that this need is a precious thing, but he can only meet that need by resisting it while the imagination is at work. Only by attending to one tension alone, one work and one witness, can the artist make the right preparation for the need of many, of perhaps all.

In every genuine artist the first care is to use his gift in such a way as to satisfy his imaginative need. If the whole world applauds a work and it does not meet this need, the work, from the point of view of the artist, is a failure. A shallow artist is disheartened by failure, but a profound one is more likely to be disheartened by success.

Art must have something of the bounty, and waste, and irregularity of life itself. Its growth is of a paradoxical kind. It may die of too much attention, and it may thrive by oppression; it may turn to the sun, but only to cast a shadow not found on any sundial. Its direction is more intricate than the direction of wind or plough, and its seasons travel across time in a different cycle. The one constant offered to the mind is unity within the possibilities of form, and this is what determines the artist's or poet's choice, the outline of his work. It is impossible to pay too much attention to form, which is the vehicle of communication; but form itself must wait upon luck to make it live; it is always an accident which gives permanence. It is this, giving unity and intensity at once, which enables the work to renew itself centuries later.

I am convinced that the foundation of art is joy. In the visual arts, in poetry and in music, the act of creation is joy. This is true, whether the work is tragic or gay or even bitter. The tragedies of Shakespeare are full of joy, reaching its highest expression. Certainly this creative joy is of a unique kind. One might think that the artists who are given it should be happy, but often they are not. There is a tension between their own values and those of the world, there is often poverty, there is the failure to satisfy the demands of the imagination, then the arid spaces between one work and another, the gulf between desire and achievement. Yet, in spite of these, in the act of creative work an artist is, and always has been, drawing from joy.

A picture, like any work of art, is an interpretation of life. Life is a miracle, and art becomes a miracle when it is a perfect refraction of life. There must be a refraction of life for art to exist, a stylisation or synthesis, if you like, of living experience. The more extreme the refraction, the more abstract art becomes; but the elements of life are still in the artist's pencil or brush. A photograph comes from the retina of the camera, an abstract picture from the retina of the mind. Before the invention of the camera, the communication of detail and of exact likeness, particularly in portraiture, had a narrative and historical value: the painter or sculptor was the visual historian of the age. That was only his subordinate role. In a great master his idiom as an artist always predominated over his subject. Now the necessity of the subordinate role has disappeared, and the artist has greater freedom of choice and of emphasis in the realm of form. In many visual artists the necessity of narrative has given way to the manipulation of motive forces, and to the excitement of form itself.

Appreciation of the Past is not enough; alone, it breeds nothing but imitation. Only a complete vision, of Past and Present, makes a work robust; a nostalgic style is the mark of the amateur. Those who have built tradition have always begun by challenging it; their work at first seemed revolutionary. The miraculous moment of composition occurs where tradition and innovation meet.

It is true that the necessity of communicating has been the germ of superlative works of art. Mozart, on his way to Prague for the first performance of *Don Giovanni*, was able in a garden to compose unforgettable arias. Music has many examples where the invitation of performance drew from the composer works which might not have existed without that prompting, and which it is difficult to imagine altered or surpassed. Music cannot indeed be separated from the idea of performance in the way that poetry can; its very composition is identified with instruments and players. Only in dramatic poetry is there an instant demand for such resources, a demand which Shakespeare, like Mozart, could meet at a moment's notice. Lyric poetry, which need not consider performers, is concerned with the kind of truth of which every performance or recital can only be an imperfect copy, as it sings its way down the generations.

Performance, then, the public form of communication, which is an opportunity to the composer of music, is a hindrance to the poet. The poet's preoccupation must remain with the secrecy of his material, the voice of articulation speaking from the subject obsessing him, of which all reproduction is only an echo. Yet the secondary thing, the reading aloud of a poem, *will* reproduce the period of composition and its excitement, however imperfectly. Such performance is nearly always disappointing to the poet himself.

In spite of this, and whatever the ingenuities of typography, poetry is written for no other purpose than to be read aloud or sung. He who looks at a poem without hearing it in his head is only half reading it. He is only receiving the poem's shape and its utility as information. If a piece of music were played by a silent orchestra, it could still be heard through a score; and the lines of a poem are such a score. They are utterance, whether read aloud or not.

Of all the arts the most immediate in its power to communicate is the dance. It is also the art in which, more than in any other, performance may surpass all that was preconceived. In music there is a momentary delay between its execution and the response. In the visual arts, painting, sculpture, architecture, although the impact is direct, its true reception is gradual and complex, for it operates on many levels. The painting, the carving or the building makes its first impact as an arrangement by the artist, but this is almost at once related to the artist's other work, to his country, to the kind of sensibility he possesses. It makes a simultaneous impact as an event in the history of art, a qualification or restatement of tradition. Only gradually, after being seen again and again, does it establish a distant identity, except in the eyes of a child.

What happened when, after Michelangelo's labours, the doors of the Sistine Chapel were opened? Was anyone among those who entered able to seize more than a fraction of the imaginative power displayed there? Was even the single design of a figure wholly accessible? Yet, when a work of art is released, its first impact will always be significant, however much this may be corrected later by seeing or hearing it again. The audience or public may be mistaken, but they cannot be deceived. There have been many instances in the past of works of genius finding at first a hostile response on all sides, but the vehemence of that response has usually indicated a recognition of their power, and a fear of conforming to it. Often an artist speaks to a generation beyond his own. As Ezra Pound has said, "Artists are the antennae of the race."

It seems to me that in our age there is, except in the first poets and artists, a much greater understanding of effect, and particularly of initial effect, than of permanence. Permanence itself is suspect in the eyes and minds of many artists, as they believe that all is flux. This is only half true. Wherever intuitive truth is manifested, though the work be hundreds or thousands of years old, eternity is present, and the dead artist who made it is revealed as our contemporary. A supreme work of art is able to persuade us that it is drawn from a timeless source, that it has existed forever, and that it is we, who believed in the fugitive nature of time, who were deceived.

Vernon Watkins 1963

The Place and the Poem

The excitement of a place is one thing, the excitement of a poem another; and the excitement of a place in a poem is a third thing, distinct from either.

Places have made a deep impression on poets, and for different reasons. Sometimes they are cherished because they hold together the memories of people, or of childhood. Those ideas and those people which time may have dispersed are recalled when the familiar place is entered; they return to a pattern, like fragments in a kaleidoscope. Dorset is made vivid through the poems of Hardy, Shropshire through those of A. E. Housman. Yet the Shropshire of Housman's poetry is a Shropshire he hardly knew as a traveller, though he saw it in his mind's eye more clearly than anyone. Read the poems first, and you will never see Shropshire as it existed before those poems were written. A place is altered by a poem. The appeal of a place may come from long associations and from memory, but sometimes it comes from the imagination alone. That is how Yeats' poem 'Byzantium' was written. He sailed to Byzantium to see with his own eyes what had so long haunted his imagination, a place which possessed for him a particular mystery that he was anxious to unfold. And Andrew Marvell, who never sailed to the Bermudas, has made those islands vivid in an unforgettable poem. He seems to have seen and passed them in his mind's eye more clearly than if he had been sailing in the boat he describes.

Memory itself works very intricately. In childhood especially we cannot choose the moments we remember afterwards. Between the deep breaths and the significant moments, ((moments, perhaps, in which a step has been taken by the will), episodes and half-episodes are photographed obliquely: a hundred thousand moments of transience are recorded in minute detail. At first they look like small coloured pictures stuck in a scrap-book by someone with no discrimination. The Swansea of my childhood's scrapbook, so much of which has been destroyed, is full of such pictures. Two or three will appear almost simultaneously at the corner of a particular street as I pass it; in one road I see a great cart-horse slipping on ice and finally falling; then I hear the noise of an iron hoop, and heels clattering. These pictures in their isolation have no value; they have not even the fluctuating value of stamps in a stamp-album. Yet any one picture, if it could be seen completely, would restore an entire world. At whatever moment the picture was taken, it remains a key to life as you knew it at that moment. Memory makes no use of such moments until, by accident, as in a poem, they fall into a pattern.

How, then does a poem about a place come to be

written? A poet, however much a place moves him, is never really able to say: 'I shall one day write a poem about this'; for appreciation is not enough in poetry. The best he can say is: 'Here is something I shall not forget'. Then, one day, when his intention to write a poem has been abandoned, the place will return by accident, and a poem about it will be written.

You will realize by this time that I am speaking from my own experience. I can speak with authority about my own poetry, and I know that wherever a place has entered my poetry it has asserted itself in this way. I want to read two poems. Both were written when the accumulated intention to write them had been abandoned; both returned to me in the form of an accident. I find that in my own poetry the pattern of a place is best recovered through a personality. I am now thinking of the two poems, the one springing from memory, the other from imagination, both about Swansea, and both suggested by a woman's death.

I came to Swansea when I was six, and within a year or two I was going to the old Uplands Cinema regularly every Saturday afternoon. It stood at the corner of the Grove until fairly recently when it was pulled down to make way for a furniture store. In the old days it used to be protected by a railing which seemed to have been built specially to keep the Saturday mob at bay. It was the time of the silent film, and the chief excitement every week was the serial, the short, horrifying serial, the nerve-tester which left every boy and girl gasping and yet hilarious when the words TO BE CONTINUED NEXT WEEK flashed upon a situation which knew of no continuation. At that moment the villain always had the upper hand. The walls of his trap-door dungeon were closing upon our hero and heroine, or knives were coming out of those walls all round them leaving one space for the final knife to come, or they were on fire, or drowning in water which was gradually filling their cell. Logically they would die, and the funeral would be on Monday. Illogically they always managed to survive, and on the following Saturday we were all there to hail their unexplained, hair-breadth escape.

More than half of the Saturday afternoon audience were children. Nearly always a few boys were thrown out, but this never happened during the serial. Throughout the serial everyone was rigid and nothing was safe as we watched the heroine gradually approaching that inextricable position of nightmare which ended each episode.

The first Great War had broken out, and we were full of stories of heroism; but the heroine of many of those serials was Pearl White, the American actress who could express horror with wider eyes than anyone else, and who really used to throw herself off buildings into rivers and risk her life in the making of the films. She was always my heroine, and I looked to her to do all the heroics which I knew I would not dare to do myself, and felt a vicarious sense of achievement when she performed them. Her name became the centre of many fights and struggles.

I grew up out of her memory. Then, one day more than twenty years later – in 1938, I think it was – I suddenly heard of her death, and the poem which I had always owed to her came to me at once. When I had finished it, I called it Elegy on the Heroine of Childhood – In Memory of Pearl White.

That poem as printed in July, 1939, just two months before the outbreak of the last war. Now I am going to turn from the poem of memory to the poem of imagination. This second poem emerges from a ruined Swansea, from a particular street in my mind's eye animated by a particular tragedy which I did not witness, though it was vividly described to me by a friend who saw it happen. This poem is called *The Spoils of War*. It has a simple and true story. In one of the air-raids on Swansea a woman left her air-raid shelter to fetch a cushion for her child who was crying and could not sleep. The woman was instantly killed by a bomb.

THE SPOILS OF WAR

The world is weaned from this one dead by the thread of
 a shawl,
How little a pin
Unfastening the fold and fuse of light in Lucifer's fall;
The world is weaned from a point in the estuary of the
 grail,
This pin, this point over and under the Bristol Channel's
 wailing,
Piercing the sky carried in the breast, flung to the maniac
 grin
Of brains and shattered windows. A mad child sucks at
 her wall.

She sprang, luminous on a wish, to the trivial
Tread of her gallows-drop, reaching for a cushion for her
 child in the shelter to sleep on,
Carved her own tombstone, then all the stars ran in
And the world shot back like a ball;

Dropping from nowhere through a whirlwind of skies and
  eyes,
Casting the vesture and tidings of those calamities,
To a shrouded, most mute place, to her inmost call
And the pavings, crying they were crossed, ring out
In a skipping-rope world of to-morrow's names and
  games,
That they were crossed, crossed, certainly crossed by the
  same,
Same feet. O gag those echoes down, lest the bloodstains
  shout.
Cover the crypt of her footprints, running from the
  sleepless, sheltered one,
Pitched into light, under the wind and whine of bombs,
When the pavings flew up to the stars in a valley of tombs.
Night is burnt white in the dirt of a street in Manselton.
Many run past her, and five stoop over her, the faceless,
  breastless one,
The steeples unpinned from her holy shadow, in the dead
  position.
Wild weddings, peals of bells in their hard, hard eyes
  proclaim a desertion.
Wounded to the death of Earth, she forgives those restless
  ones.
Divorced from her darling, O at last no ropes are rung.
Look on her face; mine eyes dazzle; she died young.

Vernon Watkins

Vernon Watkins on Modern Poets

Modern Poetry Lectures

(September 1966)

I. INTRODUCTION: WHAT IS MODERN POETRY?

In order to define modern Poetry we must ask ourselves when it came into being. If we are in the middle of a period we must ask ourselves when that period began. We may take the present as a river, a stream of consciousness, in which those who experience it share a common speech. In that speech there are certain articulations which are memorable; and, because poetry is a formal art concerned with what is memorable, it has been traditional to look to individual poets for what, in the general confusion of language, is likely to endure. What is memorable, in style or content, varies as poets vary, but the instinct of tradition, in separating them from those whose speech or writing is less formal, has proved valid in the past, and is likely to remain valid in the future. There are, then, degrees of separation: poets are separated, by the nature of their art, from other writers; they are separated from each other, because each poet's imagination is unique and therefore makes unique demands; and they are separated from the great body of traditional poetry by being modern, that is, by sharing a consciousness of conditions and events which the poets of earlier times could only share through prophecy and vision. We have now arrived by accident at a definition of modern poetry, but it is purely historical. It is, however, the only one to be trusted.

Having arrived at this historical definition: modern poetry is poetry distinguished from poetry of the past by the time factor, by being written in the circumstances and climate of the present, we must examine authors to find whether this definition holds true in point of style. Immediately we come face to face with contradictions. There are certain poets, of whom Gerard Manley Hopkins is the most conspicuous modern example, who, by an accident of delayed publication, are suddenly found to be intensely modern, and of our time; and there are other earlier poets like John Donne, Marvell, William Blake and Shakespeare, to name only English poets, who, if they once enter the stage of modern poetry by the side doors of their own age, are found to be in many ways more modern than ourselves. Besides this, there are some poets writing in our time whose verse is isolated from contemporary experience by the very intensity of their initial drive, so that the importation of elements peculiar to our age would weaken it; and there are others whose verse draws more sustenance from ancient poets than from anything that has changed, and yet remains live and vivid, even unforgettable (e.g. Auden, Eliot, Pound, David Jones).

The historical definition, then, is insufficient, and yet we can look for no other. An anthologist, I suppose, must attempt to do so. The Faber Book of Modern Verse, when it first appeared under the editorship of Michael Roberts in 1936, was such an attempt. Rich though it is in individual examples, like all anthologies it failed. The examples remain; the theory disappears. We must look deeper.

A poet is by no means anchored to the movement in which he is represented, convenient though this may be for the critic and necessary for the superficial needs of the anthologist. It is through his means of self-renewal that a poet exists at all, and those means are extremely intricate and deep-rooted. The freshness of a great poem is astonishing, but the roots are there. We cannot understand the magic of that freshness; it is too quick for analysis. We can only touch the roots from which it came. T. S. Eliot, for instance, in speaking about his own poetry, said that without the work of the French Symbolist poets of the 18th Century it would be unthinkable and would never have come into being; and here he was speaking of roots. Yeats, at the end of his life, defied anyone to call him original, since he hated originality, as it conflicted with his sole aim in poetry of restating heroic and traditional truths, copying in present-day idiom the unchanging wisdom of the past. Here, again, Yeats was speaking of roots. The inexplicable magic of the luck which makes a poem permanent was beyond discussion.

The use of contemporary idiom in speech is certainly a factor in determining what is modern in poetry. Yeats himself infused much of the gusto and strength of living Irish speech into his later poems, and the consequence of this is that they are not only much greater than the early poems, for he had then found himself, but much more modern. What, then, about Milton? When 'Paradise Lost' was published, was he modern? I return to my historical definition and say Yes. He was so modern as to reduce that word to a very small size. Modern poetry is bound to be, in any one age, the enduring achievements of the poets of one time.

II. STYLE

It has always been an axiom of mine that a true style cannot be learnt from a contemporary. I am not suggesting that poets living at the same time cannot help each other; they can do this, profoundly, but they cannot teach a style. Style is, I believe, a root thing, and roots do not run along the surface of letters. Although poetry is always, in one sense, revolutionary, because it takes the reader by surprise, it is always its relation to the past that gives depth. Since a poet is a witness, carrying news of his time to future generations, it would seem that the sharper and clearer his perceptions are, the more acute and lasting will be his findings; and yet, if clarity is the only criterion, his function will serve no better than a camera, and his art will be journalism. The perceptions of a poet must be composite, as he is a witness for the living and the dead at the same time. If he observes the two responsibilities, he will begin to see what is ancient in the contemporary scene and what is contemporary in the ancient; and his style will emerge from that collision, from that twofold perception. Only gradually does a poet find and begin to realize his particular task, for the task of each poet is different, and his true affinities in the poetry of past ages are not quickly understood. Style which has depth is recognized at once as it has immediacy, and also the corroboration of past ages; but among contemporaries it is distinction and opposition that foster style. True and different talents may feed each other, but they can only do so by obeying deep-rooted affinities, and by a divergence of style. The most fruitful relationship between contemporary poets is where a fundamental difference of style exists to serve a single truth, which then has more than one manifestation, or different truths which are bound together by affinity and indissoluble respect and affection.

If we look back through the centuries of our poetry we shall find many examples of these fruitful oppositions, of two poets innately and fundamentally different in idiom and style, but often bound by friendship and a common theme, whose work has been strengthened, not by competition, but by the assurance and expectation of works from a complementary talent. I think of Hopkins and Bridges, Browning and Landor, Shelley and Byron, Wordsworth and Coleridge, Shakespeare, Marlowe and Ben Jonson, to name only a few; and European poetry is equally rich in these examples. Lyrically every poet is alone. Style is a root thing; development is something which unfolds.

When the imagination of a poet is awakened, he is aware of infinite possibilities. The scope of creative possibility is boundless until it encounters the restraint of style. Style may be called a curb, a deliberate or instinctive choice among countless alternatives, and in poetry the choice lies in word, phrase, metric and cadence. A poet may exercise his talent by trying to grasp all possibilities at once; he may try to herd together an almost infinite number of rapidly moving ideas in an inconclusive poem. He will fail, because style teaches that only in minute particulars can remote and separate things be harnessed, and perception find its reward. Style, then, whose function it is to reduce infinite possibilities to finite form, is the highest thing of which an artist is capable, as it serves the purpose of revealing the essential qualities of everything it isolates, and is able to say by implication more than it can even comprehend.

There are as many distinctions of style as there are good poets, but certain broad categories may be recognized.

In poetry a rhetorical style is one in which accuracy of statement combines with force and resonance to produce a single effect. Rhetoric is defined as the art of using language to persuade or influence others; but in verse one has to be more specific. Oratory, which uses rhetoric for persuasion in addressing others, must be distinguished from poetry, which uses rhetoric to persuade the poet himself; for the poet, in writing his poem, is a listener, and not a speaker. As Yeats has written, 'We may make out of the quarrel with others, rhetoric, but of the quarrel with ourselves, poetry.' ('Per Amica Silentia Lunae' in 'Mythologies' (Macmillan, 1959). Even if you think of an orator preparing and practicing his speech and trying out its effects on himself, that is not the same process as verse composition, because the poet is awaiting his own persuasion as he writes; he is not persuaded already. He may know the dominant truth of his poem, but if he did not expect more than the reason could anticipate, he would write in prose. The unpredictable addition is peculiar to language and to style, and only labour, patience and experiment will find it. The finding of rhetorical statement exactly fitted to his own verse is peculiar to each poet. Therefore to dismiss rhetoric in verse involves a great many dismissals. The rhetoric of Marlowe is one thing, the rhetoric of Milton another. Take away rhetoric from one poet's work, and the loss will be tremendous; add it to another's, and the work will become false or affected. Rhetoric is no criterion of goodness or badness; everything depends on whether it is necessary to a poet's style.

A laconic or suggestive style is the opposite of the rhetorical. This found many examples among the French symbolist poets of the nineteenth century, one of whom, Paul Verlaine, in his 'Art Poetique', advised poets to take rhetoric and wring its neck. An art arose in which symbols, rather than rhetoric, displayed power; and the secret of power lay in the arrangement of symbols projected by poets, and the mood and feelings which they evoked, rather than in any abstract kind of persuasion of thought. The early poetry of Yeats was influenced by this, and so was the early poetry of Eliot.

A colloquial style was often incorporated in the suggestive style of the French Symbolist poets. Slang and dialect and staccato speech rhythms became the equipment of Tristan Corbière, used in his poems, but in the artifice of form these poets were considerable masters; speech rhythms were harnessed to an extremely exact metric and structure. Stephane Mallarmé, who was a master of rhyme, sought a return to Orpheus, to the magic of language itself, before the sophistication of literature. Eliot transposed a line of one of Mallarmé's sonnets ('Le Tombeau d'Edgar Poe') in 'Little Gidding': 'To purify the dialect of the tribe.' Mallarmé thought of rhetoric as remote and alien to immediate experience, and he broke down syntax in order to create the lost immediacy, as Orpheus plucked timeless notes on his lyre, from the magic properties of words. Corbière and Mallarmé both found their way into Eliot's work; and through the help of Arthur Symons, the poet and translator, Yeats became, in the middle nineties, when they had adjoining lodgings in the Temple, well acquainted with the poetry of Mallarmé and Verlaine. Yeats, in 'The Winding Stair' (1933), wrote this poem:

THE NINETEENTH CENTURY AND AFTER
Though the great song return no more
There's keen delight in what we have:
The rattle of pebbles on the shore
Under the receding wave.

And nobody had a clearer vision than Yeats of the bitter, staring disillusionment behind much of the poetry written in our time. His most condensed statement on this subject is found in another poem from 'The Winding Stair':

THREE MOVEMENTS
Shakespearean fish swam the sea, far away from land;
Romantic fish swam in nets coming to the hand;
What are all those fish that lie gasping on the strand?

The Poetry of W. B. Yeats

Introduction to Lecture at York and Hull

I have yet to read a study of W. B. Yeats' poetry at all adequate to its subject. In 1960, when the criticism of poetry is so stream-lined that a poet has hardly died before all his reasons for living are explained away, Yeats remains, not only the supreme poet of our age, but the one most difficult to synthesize and to assess.

There are, I think, three reasons for this. First, Yeats renewed himself at each stage of his life. It was, as A. E. observed, his habit of intellectual adventure that kept his poetry fresh, and, however eccentric those excursions of his intensely abstract mind were, they were invariably dedicated to self-renewal.

Secondly, himself a sensitive and religious man, and in youth inclined to be timid, he was dominated by the heroic mask of others, and cast himself in the role of Hero. His own saintlike conscience was turned to his father, whose agnostic love of art opposed all that was conventional, whether in life or idea; to Synge, a man of hatred and fierce indignation, who sang to the last the joy of exuberant life of which bad health had deprived him; to Lady Gregory, who on her deathbed placed her faith in the poetry which came from original sin. It was Swift, a figure of heroic isolation, who was in old age the teacher of his own hatred and his indignation at the Irish political scene.

The third reason is likely to prove the greatest obstacle to commentators. Yeats trusted, in everything he wrote, the moment which was most difficult to analyse, and it was this supernatural moment, he argued, that gave the poem permanence. Reason may split hairs, but the hair that is split when reason has finished is the lyrical element, and perhaps no poet worked more diligently or with more patience to find it.

It is about the poetry that I am going to speak, but I should like to quote here two passages from the late prose. 'We must not make a false faith by hiding from our thoughts the causes of doubt, for faith is the highest achievement of the human intellect, the only gift man can make to God, and therefore it must be offered in sincerity.'

The second passage is from Yeats' Introduction to one of the Upanishads (the Mandukya Upanishad), published in 1935:

> 'The Heart is unity, harmony. The Mind is no more to be occupied with external events, it must, it seems, turn upon itself, be occupied with itself, but that is impossible, for the Discursive Mind must by its nature pursue something, find something.'

Yeats was conscious of the necessity of an audience, but all his poetry was beaten out by the conflict of a dialogue with himself, the results of which were awaited by a permanent audience for poetry, which he estimated at the number of a thousand souls.

Yes, Yeats really did say those words about a poem being 'a piece of luck'... unless my memory deceives me, and it rarely does about such things. He had talked at length about the great difficulty of getting a poem right, about its nearly being there. 'And then', he said, and he flicked his fingers as he said it, 'you get the luck.'

Thomas Hardy

Hardy would have been more complete if he had been more physical… but it is often metaphysical grip that his poems lack. He is, at his best, a superb poet, and there's nobody like him.

Hardy's poems are often right in relation to fact and anecdote, and right because they have a kind of aura belonging to his sensibility, but poetically they are often wrong, because they leave the imagination with misgiving, remorse, the opposite of imagination's food.

And Hardy didn't revise in Yeats' way, because I think he had a novelist's mind, though a poet's instinct.

A. E. Housman

The poetry of A. E. Housman depends for its existence on a rejection of the terms offered by life when youth has gone. Joy itself cannot, for Housman, be lost more than once, for the loss of that first freshness of life, like unrequited love, is for him irretrievable and final. There can be no development, only the celebration of bravery and fidelity; and the rest of life to the very point of death must be faced with stoic heroism. No poet of comparable gifts ever denied himself progress so ruthlessly, or opposed his own sensuous nature with such an unwavering will. His intellectual power, which was considerable, he regarded as a hindrance rather than a help to his poetry, and the most adventurous and searching part of it he kept away from his crystalline verse, lest it should cloud the issue.

In 1933, three years before his death at the age of seventy-six, Housman broke a long silence when he delivered at Cambridge his lecture on 'The Name and

Nature of Poetry'. This lecture is full of examples of the highest poetry, whose miraculous nature transcends thought and remains inexplicable, and of other examples which Housman sees as poetry mixed with thought and sentiment, esteemed as much, Housman feels, for the thought and sentiment, which could be expressed in prose, as for the poetry itself. He writes: 'Poems very seldom consist of poetry and nothing else; and pleasure can also be derived from their other ingredients. I am convinced that most readers, when they think that they are admiring poetry, are deceived by inability to analyse their sensations, and that they are really admiring, not the poetry of the passage before them, but something else in it, which they like better than poetry.' Housman's attitude is explicably stated early in the essay: 'I think that to transfuse emotion – not to transmit thought but to set up in the reader's sense a vibration corresponding to what was felt by the writer- is the peculiar function of poetry.'

There is, then, in Housman's art, not only the limitation of his Spartan and stoic attitude to life, but a second limitation in the art itself, and the two are interdependent. The first limitation imposes on the art a restraint of subject, and the second, by excluding developing thought, keeps the subject in its first intensity of feeling, like a perfectly formed vessel in which the smouldering incense burns to dust.

Between 1896, when Housman published 'A Shropshire Lad', and 1922, when his 'Last Poems' appeared, no great change is discernable either in the life or in the work. The Latin scholar pursued his lectures and textual researches at Cambridge, and treated every example of bad scholarship in his fellow researchers with withering contempt. Yet the last poems were as free from the interference of alien themes as their predecessors twenty-six years before. The craftsmanship was, if anything, more perfect, and in the lyric notes as limpid and pure as ever. The posthumous collection of 'More Poems', which does not reflect Housman's personal choice, has several perfect poems, a greater part being unequal to his best, but in a few of 'Last Poems' there are, I think, certain key elements and subtleties belonging to rhythm as much as to language which make them surpass all in 'A Shropshire Lad'; but the character of all is the same.

The two books of verse which Housman published, separated in their dates by so long a period, were made to fit the pocket, and they immediately reached a wide and devoted public. Nowhere else in English poetry could this particular lyric note be heard, and it was unmistakable. Soldiers of the First World War carried the small 'Shropshire Lad' volume in the trenches, not only because of the courage and self-sacrifice contained in many of the poems, but because Housman found a voice for their own feelings, simple, forceful and true, a voice which offered them, in a time of trouble, not comfort, but an alternative to despair.

What, we may finally ask, is the secret of Housman's lyric power? It is derived, I think, from three sources, which he co-ordinated to perfection. The first is an economy and directness of diction which he learnt from Milton and Blake, the latter of whom he placed as a lyric poet next to Shakespeare, and from the Latin and Greek poets. The second is a simplicity and magic of cadence, which he learnt perhaps from Heine, whom he admired and with whom he has so much affinity in both texture and theme. The third is more elusive. It is an ancestral gift, although its ancestry is hidden, a pictorial gift of condensation. Everywhere in Housman's verse is found the power to evoke, by the simplest and shortest words, landscape and situation in relation to man, and to 'the troubles of our proud and angry dust'; and in this poetry the poignancy of situation persists, for the conflict between man's affection and his destiny, between his heroic will and the silence of eternity, is never resolved.

Siegfried Sassoon

Siegfried Sassoon is the one poet emerging from the First World War to become the prophet of the Second, and then, surviving the Second, to beat his weapon of protest into a mirror of meditation, who has finally hidden even that mirror on the altar of worship. In the work of David Jones, who has an affinity of war experience, the acts of war, reflected and transfigured in his own mirror of meditation, still vibrate and have their symbolic place in religious observance. I can think of no other example, for Wilfred Owen is dead.

Although Owen died at twenty-five, killed within a week of the 1918 Armistice, he had already come under the influence of Siegfried Sassoon, who was his senior Officer, so deeply that several of his poems, like 'Conscious' and 'The Next War', carry the hallmark of Sassoon's own war poetry, both in protest and warning. Even the fragmentary Preface which was found after Owen's death and which Sassoon, as editor, quoted in full in the first edition of his friend's poems, seems to echo the voices of both poets. And unquestionably poems like 'The Chances' and 'Disabled', which have the unmistakeable timbre of Owen's voice, are related to Sassoon's own poetry of protest. 'The Chances', like another of Wilfred Owen's poems, 'Mental Cases', deals with madness, 'Disabled' with the physical mutilation of war. 'Disabled' was written in 1917. In October of that year Sassoon himself showed it to Robert Graves. Here is its opening:

> He sat in a wheeled chair, waiting for dark,
> And shivered in his ghastly suit of grey,
> Legless, sewn short at elbow. Through the park
> Voices of boys rang saddening like a hymn,
> Voices of play and pleasure after day,
> Till gathering sleep had mothered them from him.

and it ends:

> Some cheered him home, but not as crowds cheer Goal.
> Only a solemn man who brought him fruits
> *Thanked* him; and then inquired about his soul.
>
> Now, he will spend a few sick years in Institutes,
> And do what things the rules consider wise,
> And take whatever pity they may dole.
> To-night he noticed how the women's eyes
> Passed from him to the strong men that were whole.
> How cold and late it is! Why don't they come
> And put him into bed? Why don't they come?

The poem 'Does it Matter', by Sassoon, is also dated 1917:

> Does it matter? – losing your legs?...
> For people will always be kind,
> And you need not show that you mind
> When the others come in after football
> To gobble their muffins and eggs.
>
> Does it matter? – losing your sight?...
> There's such splendid work for the blind;
> And people will always be kind,
> As you sit on the terrace remembering
> And turning your face to the light.
>
> Do they matter? – those dreams from the pit?...
> You can drink and forget and be glad,
> And people won't say that you're mad;
> For they'll know that you've fought for your country,
> And no one will worry a bit.

The two poets knew each other, not only in France, but at Craiglockhart War Hospital, near Edinburgh, to which both were invalided home, and there they showed each other poems. How close they were to each other at this time, both in thought and expression, may be seen in many poems. The theme of 'the Future forgetting the dead in War', which Owen had noted in his plan for a book of his poems which he never lived to see, governed many examples. Sassoon's 'Song-Books of the War' is a poem which looks ahead from 1917 to our own day, imagining boys who, hearing songs of the war, are filled with envy of those 'lads who fought in France and lived in time to share the fun.' But Owen's 'Miners', written a few months later, in its close allows those whom war has buried to speak:

Comforted years will sit soft-chaired
  In rooms of amber;
The years will stretch their hands, well-cheered
  By our lives' ember.
The centuries will burn rich loads
  With which we groaned,
Whose warmth shall lull their dreaming lids
  While songs are crooned.
But they will not dream of us poor lads
  Lost in the ground.

Again, Owen's satirical poem 'Inspection' in which blood on a uniform has been objected to as dirt, and which ends with the soldier's comment to the officer:

'But when we're duly white-washed, being dead,
The race will bear Field Marshal God's Inspection.'

—this poem bears a close resemblance to several of Sassoon's poems, both in construction and language, particularly to his poem 'They', in which the Bishop says the boys will be changed when they come home:

'We're none of us the same,' the boys reply.
'For George lost both his legs; and Bill's stone blind;
And Bert's gone syphilitic: you'll not find
A chap who's served that hasn't found *some* change.'
And the Bishop said: 'The ways of God are strange!'

While I think of these poems of Sassoon belonging to the last years of that war, I recognize a satirical edge unrivalled by any other poet of the time. They were written in the middle of experience in which he played an heroic part, and from which he saw the future as the road to ruin, unless a sublime alternative were to be found. Their influence on Owen is evident. I take one more example. The third verse of Owen's poem 'A Terre' begins:

A short life and a merry one, my buck!
We used to say we'd hate to live dead-old,-
But now... I'd willingly be puffy, bald
And patriotic...

And here is Sassoon's 'Base Details':

If I were fierce and bald and short of breath,
I'd live with scarlet Majors at the Base,
And speed glum heroes up the line to death.
You'd see me with my puffy petulant face
Guzzling and gulping in the best hotel,
Reading the Roll of Honour; 'Poor young chap,'
I'd say – 'I used to know his father well;
Yes, we've lost heavily in this last scrap.'
And when the war is done and youth stone dead,
I'd toddle safely home and die – in bed.

Even Owen's punning titles for the poems 'Spring Offensive' and 'The Dead-Beat' have something in common with Sassoon's method in 'Base Details'. When the ironic and satirical element is abandoned, the two poets are very different, both lyrically and in thought.

Their differences are evident in Wilfred Owen's poem 'Asleep' and Sassoon's 'The Dug-Out'. Here is Owen's poem:

ASLEEP

Under his helmet, up against his pack,
After the many days of work and waking,
Sleep took him by the brow and laid him back.
And in the happy no-time of his sleeping,
Death took him by the heart. There was a quaking
Of the aborted life within him leaping...
Then chest and sleepy arms once more fell slack.
And soon the slow, stray blood came creeping
From the intrusive lead, like ants on track.

***

Whether his deeper sleep lie shaded by the shaking
Of great wings, and the thoughts that hung in the stars,
High-pillowed on calm pillows of God's making
Above these clouds, these rains, these sleets of lead,
And these winds' scimitars;
-Or whether yet his thin and sodden head
Confuses more and more with the low mould,
His hair being one with the grey grass
And finished fields of autumns that are old...
Who knows? Who hopes? Who troubles? Let it pass!
He sleeps. He sleeps less tremulous, less cold
Than we who must awake, and waking, say Alas!

And here is Sassoon's poem:

THE DUG-OUT

Why do you lie with your legs ungainly huddled,
And one arm bent across your sullen cold
Exhausted face? It hurts my heart to watch you,
Deep-shadow'd from the candle's guttering gold:
And you wonder why I shake you by the shoulder;
Drowsy you mumble and sigh and shift your head...
You are too young to fall asleep for ever;
And when you sleep you remind me of the dead.

The common ground of indignation and compassion is in both poems, but the means producing their effect have little in common. Owen uses touch throughout, Sassoon only once. In Owen's poem the helmet, the head on the pack, 'the slow, stray blood' creeping 'from the intrusive lead like ants on track', then 'these winds' scimitars', and the head laid on the mould, 'the hair being one with the grey grass': all these are tactile images and causes. Sassoon's poem is not tactile, in spite of the one line in which he shakes the young soldier by the shoulder; it is made of music and light, and it uses lilt and cadence for its effects. The whole composition is musical, and in a subtle way abstracted from the actual experience, whereas Owen's speech is plastic throughout.

Both these poems, Sassoon's 'The Dug-Out' and Owen's 'Asleep', have a black background. In Sassoon's poem the soldier is asleep; in Owen's he is dead. Owen moves out into the territory of darkness to find the stars, while Sassoon is held back by his love of the living, his allegiance to life. It is not only the subject that determines this difference. Sassoon is indignant that war has broken the harmony of Earth and killed the landscape he was born to, now invaded by horror and deformity. Owen is indignant with the landscape which has cheated us. He is concerned with chaos, while Sassoon is revolted by it. In Sassoon's poem death is despair, it is falling asleep forever; in Owen's the despair lies rather in continuing to live in those terrible conditions from which death is a release; despair is left as the property of those who survive the soldier.

'Above all,' wrote Owen in his fragmentary Preface which he intended to publish with his poems, 'this book is not concerned with poetry. My subject is War, and the pity of war. The poetry is in the pity.' And Sassoon, in his preface to Owen's first posthumous collection, wrote that some academically-minded people would be more interested in the experiments Owen made in assonance and dissonance than in the profound humanity of the poet's soul. Both statements are aimed at all that is esoteric in art, and it seems that both these poets were so embittered and disillusioned by their war experience that they revolted against the very idealism and nostalgia of poetry and music which gave them their first impulse to write. For poetry was to Owen what music was to Sassoon. In Owen's poem 'A Terre' the mortally wounded soldier says:

> I have my medals? – Discs to make eyes close.
> My glorious ribbons? – Ripped from my own back
> In scarlet shreds. (That's for your poetry book.)

The sardonic note cannot be mistaken. And if we look for it in Sassoon we have only to turn to his poem 'Dead Musicians', beginning:

From you, Beethoven, Bach, Mozart
  The substance of my dreams took fire.
You built cathedrals in my heart,
  And lit my pinnacled desire.

which ends, after the interruption of a soldier's ragtime song:

And so the song breaks off; and I'm alone.
They're dead... For God's sake stop that gramophone.

Without such moments of revolt how can the quarrel of life and art ever be truly resolved? An art is rejected only to be reaffirmed on a deeper level, and it is precisely this rejection that marks Owen's maturity and the beginning of Sassoon's later development. While the war still raged, both poets banished all the academic manifestations of their favourite arts from the circle of experience, the fiery furnace into which Necessity had thrown them as witnesses. It was Sassoon who survived, and Owen prophesied this, when he wrote, at the very end of the second version of 'A Terre', which he dedicated to Siegfried Sassoon under the title 'Wild With All Regrets':

I think on your rich breathing, brother, I'll be weaned
To do without what blood remained me from my wound.

A Note on D. H. Lawrence

When I read D. H. Lawrence's poems, I am aware always of a man in conflict. The conflict belongs first to the nature of the man which is passionate with a kind of unresolved passion, revolutionary yet hating every reform, worshipping the intensity of the body, exalting it without sensuality, filled at once with idealism and rage, idealism of the body and rage against all the forces which have attempted to mechanize it, to subdue it. Lawrence valued the body and the senses more than the mind. He did not look for the translation of physical sensations into the metaphysical and rarified atmosphere of spiritual ideas which is found so often in the poetry of Rilke; he looked for the apotheosis of the senses themselves, and of the body. He believed that the body was sacred and in flux, like the whole of creation; at one time the bond of union between the physical body and all nature in the world has been magical and timeless, but the thread had been cut; the magical body of firelight and the primeval forest had been lost and the enslaved body and the factory were taking their place.

Lawrence loved the order of primitive creation, he found ecstasy in the grace and energy and movement of naked uncivilized bodies, a kind of music in primitive instruments and weapons, and a deep communion existing always between the hunter and the hunted, between the killer and the killed that ancient, sacred music was dying. Where the magic of the forest and of the marshland had been, the industrial town had sprung up; the energy of men had yielded to the energy of the machine, and the poet saw the smoking factories with their jaws of steel disgorging machine after machine.

Lawrence saw the factory as a terrible idol, identified with wealth and destructive power. He hated the machine with a fanatical hatred. It was the enemy and the enemy of man.

The poems and fragments Lawrence directed against the machines and their mechanization of life, and against the refinements of the machine that bring war and what Lawrence called the 'refinements of evil', are unanswerable. The factories were the denial of all that is glorious in the senses; they were the 'dark, Satanic mills' of Blake's 'Jerusalem', – of Blake, who also exalted the senses and found divinity in the perceptions. 'Everything that lives is holy', Blake sang. And Lawrence saw everything unholy that restrained or obstructed or darkened the freedom of the life of the senses. There the resemblance between the two poets ends, for Lawrence appears to have known nothing of the paradox which was the foundation of Blake's writing. Lawrence could not separate the subjective states of man from his objective appearance, nor could he distinguish effectively between the Natural Man and the Spiritual Man which Blake could always see as two aspects of the same individual, two separate lives running concurrently in the consciousness and in the blood. Blake knew the human heart profoundly and he understood the human brain, but Lawrence seems only to have known them by their manifestations of exuberance, which he recognized as beautiful or ugly. Lawrence saw impulse as ritualistic, keeping man with life, but intellect as a spectre leading him to barren formulation and death. His aesthetic world had no fixed centre. The centre itself was the hub of a rushing wheel, it was moving as the cosmos was moving. He would not accept 'Truth'; truth itself was moving. This partly explains why he never completed a poem, in the word's true meaning, unless it was a poem about a *part* of nature; and it wholly explains why his poetry has so much emotional force but lacks spiritual authority and power.

On T. S. Eliot

(for 'The Direct Eyes' Television 10th January, 1965)

Eliot was always conscious of the moment of death. 'We are born with the dead', he says in 'Little Gidding', and again in 'The Dry Salvages'; 'And the time of death is every moment'.

He was full of gaiety and humour. You could not imagine a more sympathetic and responsive person. He knew all about despair: he had explored it to the utmost. And he was wholly dedicated to life. He was prepared to help anyone who wanted help, and to give himself as completely as he could.

The excitement of Eliot's early poems, when they came out after the end of the First World War, was revolutionary. Yeats called him the most revolutionary man in poetry in his lifetime, and he was right. Eliot caught, brilliantly and exactly, the details of peoples' lives in a city, and, with his faultless ear, made them unforgettable. Suddenly everyone was quoting this new poetry; it spread like Asian 'flu, and became part of our experience. It was impossible to separate London from the evocative echoes of his work. It was impossible for any poet to escape his influence.

This influence was liberating and constricting at the same time. Eliot had broken up the formal rhythm and rhyme of regular stanzas for the sake of a new music corresponding more closely to the movement of life. He substituted an often irregular line of his own, its cadence depending on speech rhythms and the demands of his subject. He accepted everyday life as material for poetry; he banished artificial poetic diction, and tested a poem by one thing only: 'Is it genuine?'

That was very liberating and fair enough. Everyone started writing realistic poems in a looser form, out of genuine experience, and everyone was surprised to find that they were not at all like Eliot's. Therein lay the constriction. The miracle of putting down everyday life in unforgettable terms had been performed, but it could not be repeated by others. Eliot's technique – and technique is always linked with belief – was such that a thousand readings could not exhaust the poem's meaning or its charm.

I remember him saying to me that the poetry of 'Four Quartets' was better poetry than the poetry of 'The Waste Land'; but he didn't repudiate his early work. In form he never repeated himself, but he continually recreated himself in each poem, and without the early poetry, the late work, in which his lyric power reached its greatest heights, would not have been possible.

I think his influence will always be immediate, and not retrospective, and that is the mark of a great poet. Critics think in terms of decades, poets in terms of centuries. I believe that in whatever century Eliot's work is accessible, his influence will be immediate, and its effect profound.

Who can better teach how little is visible
Save in the eye of God?
Tentatively you struggled,
Mapping slowly the land we know.

T. S. ELIOT: FOUR QUARTETS

Structure: musical. 5 movements in each of the four poems. Probably most affinity in music with the late quartets of Beethoven. That in A minor, Op.132, has five movements, Op.130, the last he was to finish, has seven.

It has been pointed out that Beethoven's late quartets all radiate from a central experiment (J.W.N. Sullivan in 'Beethoven, His Spiritual Development' A Knopf, New York, 1927), and this is true also of Eliot's great poem. The fifth and final movement of 'Little Gidding' recapitulates the themes of the three earlier Quartets, just as Beethoven does in the last movement of the Ninth Symphony. Beethoven resolves his poem in 'the crowned knot of fire

And the fire and rose are one.

Beethoven's late quartets and this last Symphony are triumphant statements rising out of an almost insuperable despair and the personal affliction of his deafness. Eliot also had his despair, before his conversion to orthodox Christianity, celebrated in the poem 'Ash Wednesday'. The Four Quartets, the crown of his poetic achievement, reaffirm that celebration on many levels. The poem is concerned with time, with evil, with suffering, with the validity of prayer, with old age, with childhood, with the presence of Christ in all human life, with redemption, and with the union with God. These themes are attached to everyday life and to physical places.

Burnt Norton: a manor in Gloucestershire, with a formal garden, near which Eliot lived for some time. Eliot has said that he was unacquainted with the history of the place.

A literal translation of Heraclitus's Greek epigraph at the beginning is:

> 'Although the word is in common use for all, most men live as if each had a private wisdom of his own'. But Eliot thought this quite inadequate for the Greek. Here is an extract from one of his letters:
>
> 'Herman Diels' 'Fragments der Vorsokratiker' is, I believe, still considered the standard text of the pre-Socratic philosophers... I should say that Herakleitos meant a great deal more than simply 'the word is in common use.' I think that he meant rather that the reason, the Logos, or the rational understanding of the nature of things is common or available to all men. 'Most people live as if they had a peculiar and individual insight.' No one translation, however, can be considered as anything more than a limited interpretation since the meaning of key words in Greek philosophy can never be completely rendered in a modern language. That is my reason for putting the Greek text instead of an English translation of it. (E. M. Stephenson in 'T.S. Eliot and the Lay Reader' [Fortune Press, London, 1947]).

I transcribe Miss Stephenson's own paraphrase of a

discussion she had with Eliot on November 24th, 1943, in order to define 'the figure of the ten stairs', in Section V:

'"The figure of the ten stairs" refers to the "Bride" which is used symbolically of the Soul in its upward movement towards God. The "ladder" or "step" to which St John of the Cross refers, and which Mr Eliot uses in poetry as "stairs" signifies Divine Love and Faith.' St John's description of the Ten Degrees of the Mystical ladder of Divine Love is as follows:

'The first degree of love makes the soul languish to its great profit... As a sick man loses the desire for, and the taste of all food... so the soul in this degree of love loses all pleasures of earthly things, and all desire of them, and changes its colour, that is, the conditions of the past life. It finds no comfort, pleasure, nor support anywhere.

Second: So anxious is the soul now that it seeks the Beloved in all things; all its thought, words, and works are referred to Him; in eating, sleeping, and waking, all its anxieties are about Him.

The third step of the ladder of love renders the soul active and fervent, so that it faints not. The soul, because of the great love it has for God, is in great pain and suffering because of the scantiness of its service... it looks upon itself therefore as unprofitable in all it does, and upon its life as worthless. Another most wonderful effect is that it looks upon itself as being in truth the very worst of souls. On this third step the very soul is far from giving way to vain glory or presumption, or from condemning others.

When the soul is on the fourth step of the ladder of love, it falls into a state of suffering, but without weariness... It seeks not for consolations or sweetness either in God or elsewhere, neither does it pray for God's gifts, seeing clearly how many it has already received. For all it cares for now is how it shall please God, and serve Him, in some measure in return for His goodness, and for the graces it has received, and this at any end and every cost. This degree of love is exceedingly high.

On the fifth step of the ladder the soul longs after God, and desires Him with impatience. Great is the eagerness of the soul on this step to embrace and be united to the Beloved.

When the soul has ascended to the sixth step, it runs swiftly to God, from Whom it receives many touches; and hope, too, runs without fainting, for love has made it strong and makes it fly rapidly.

On the seventh step the soul becomes vehemently bold; in this intense and loving exaltation, no prudence can withhold it, no counsel control it, no shame restrain it; for the favour which God hath shown it has made it vehemently bold.

On the eighth step of union the desires of the soul are satisfied, but not without interruption. Some souls ascend to this step and at once fall back; if they did not, and remained there, they would have attained to a certain state of blessedness in this life, and thus the soul tarries but briefly on this step of the ladder.

On the ninth step the soul is on fire sweetly. This step is that of the perfect who burn away sweetly in God, for this sweet and delicious burning is the work of the Holy Ghost because of the union of the soul with God. St Gregory says of the Apostles that they burned interiorly with love sweetly, when the Holy Ghost descended upon them.

On the tenth step of the ladder the soul becomes wholly assimilated into God in the beatific vision which it then immediately enjoys; for having ascended in this life to the ninth, it goeth forth out of the body. For these – they are few – being perfectly purified by love, do not pass through purgatory.'

Eliot is, as a Christian, considering the ascent to God throughout 'Four Quartets', as Dante considered it throughout the 'Commedia', and certainly Dante is his model in the unrhymed terzinas which are in the second movement of 'Little Gidding'. He is also considering it from the very first words of 'Burnt Norton' to the last words of 'Little Gidding', for this is a single poem, and Eliot himself asked for it to be judged as such. It is also very closely knit in its four parts; it is far more tightly held together than 'The Waste Land'.

Primarily I commend to you Eliot's own recording of 'Four Quartets': it is the aural manuscript of the poem, and it will teach you more than any commentary can do. A great poem cannot be simplified beyond its own words; it took Eliot half a lifetime to learn those words, and paraphrase won't do.

I want, therefore, simply to point out the structure, which is most interesting and rewarding, and helps towards a true apprehension of the poem.

It is also interesting to know that a cordwainer called Andrew Eliot made, in 1637, the crossing of the Atlantic, leaving East Coker in Somerset for the fifty-day sea voyage, and becoming enrolled as a member of the First Church of Beverley, Massachusetts in 1670. From him T. S. Eliot was descended, and in East Coker his remains are now buried.

Burnt Norton is, as I have mentioned, a manor house in Gloucestershire. The Dry Salvages, Les Trois Sauvages, are three rocks on the coast of Massachusetts, to which Andrew Eliot sailed. Little Gidding is the village with the Church where Lancelot Andrews preached; and, as Neville Braybrooke has pointed out, its

> Children in the apple-tree
> Not known, because not looked for

are linked with Burnt Norton, the Gloucestershire house in which the poet discovered that 'the leaves were full of children', a reminder of even earlier still when in New Hampshire he had also heard 'children's voices in the orchard' as he stood listening and watching: (T. S. Eliot, Hart-Davis, 1958, ed. N. Braybrooke, p.14:

> Golden head, black wing,
> Cling, swing,
> Spring, sing,
> Swing up into the apple-tree.

The apple-tree represents Christ in all Christian symbolism.

Notes on Auden

Auden is far too considerable a poet to be discussed in summary fashion. He is in movement, and, in matters of form, unpredictable. He is capable of attempting almost anything.

Although an extremely accomplished poet, he is not, I think, primarily an artist but an interpreter. He is continually challenging the false positions of art in terms of life. Indeed, he makes his poems by challenging these as he goes along. His range and understanding of poetry are wide enough to take almost everything in, and to analyse very different poets with fairness and penetration.

Auden began as a scientist, and came to write poetry late in adolescence. His first instinct of a positive nature was, I think, to attack the death-wish which he found in the minds and some of the verses of others. For this he used an increasingly skilful equipment of simple, direct and ironic language, an agile wit, a natural versatility in metric forms and a deft command of rhyme. Sometimes the slang of an English prep. school, and of psychology, crept into the vocabulary. Possibly his Icelandic ancestry enabled him to mould English like a favourite foreign language, or at least to see and handle it objectively.

His early collaboration with Christopher Isherwood in writing plays helped him to extend and exercise his talents in a new medium, and this was a foretaste of his writings for opera. 'The Dog Beneath the Skin' and 'The Ascent of F. 6' enjoyed recurrent success even after the thirties, when they broke new ground in verse drama.

Auden's whole concern since his maturity has been with Christian doctrine in relation to life, and the tensions of everyday life are, in his poetry, always related to ethics. He is honest in that he is completely unpretentious. Even against his own will he has become a sage. But he is as alert as he ever was, examining and testing behaviour, and predilections, his own and other people's, against what Kierkegaard would call 'the eternal', or the category of eternal life. Auden has always insisted on living in the present; and his present, like Kierkegaard's 'Now', includes all that was real in the past and all that will be real, so far as he can perceive it, in the future. He relegates art to a rather low place. If forms of art interfere with salvation, they have to go: salvation is more important. Blake said: Prayer is the study of art. Praise is the practice of art. But these are sayings which, I think, Auden would not accept.

W. H. AUDEN

Auden shouldn't have left out [from his Collected Poems] 'Sir, No Man's Enemy'; but of course, if it irritates him, he's right. A poet must accept contradictions, contraries.

I give him 'A' for belief, 'B' for imagination, which also always needs forgiveness, and 'C' for correction. Still, he's fine, and 'The Shield of Achilles' would astound you if his initials were T. H. wouldn't it? [a reference to Philip Larkin's passion for Thomas Hardy poems.]

A Note on the Poetry of Charles Williams

To-day there is a profound misunderstanding of the nature of poetry, and of the poet's function. It is commonly imagined that a poet's conflict begins with his own time, that one poet through a heightened critical faculty can shed an illumination on it, while another through the gunpowder of his discontent seeks to undermine it. A poet is to be distinguished from the other spokesman of his time only by the nature of his articulation; his ideal language is a kind of lucid, rational, heightened prose masquerading in verse form. If he is lucky or skilful enough to catch the rhythm of natural speech he may win an audience. It is the lot of the unlucky to have recourse to tradition, to canvass the votes of the dead.

I think that poetry of this age which will live is invariably poetry that has eluded all expectations. It may have done so through a peculiar, selective imagination, through a new technique, or through a strong personal conviction. In each case the character of the poet will bring its own rewards. But it is in the nature of poetry to astonish the poet first, before it astonishes the public.

I am looking back from a new century to the poetry of this age, and although I see what seems at first a huge rubbish-heap, it is a rubbish heap of inexhaustible interest. A great deal of material has fallen into the category of poetry which does not belong to it. Then my eye falls on an object distinguished from the rest by its crystalline, self-contained symmetry. In symbolic terms it is a receptacle of imponderable light, like those glass ornaments whose intricate design one could never quite fathom, on a Christmas tree. It is, perhaps, one of Charles Williams' poems, or perhaps the whole of his poetry, for in this case the one and the many are the same.

The poetry of Charles Williams was, in any case, bound to be different, because of the difference of his gift. He was given a kind of second sight which enabled him to see everywhere, and most immediately, the recurrence of spiritual values. If he looked at a face, he saw it in many dimensions, reflecting present, past and future ages simultaneously. It was involved, like all other faces, in the conflict between good and evil; it inherited all ages, was accessible to the operation of witchcraft and the powers of grace at the same time, and he was able to invest its radiance or shadow with an extension, both in time and space. The shadow could fall across countries. The voice could speak through centuries.

Roy Campbell

The sudden and tragic death of Roy Campbell in a motoring accident in Portugal means a loss to English poetry which cannot be replaced. The contemporary poetic stage is now robbed of its most adventurous and flamboyant figure. Ever since 1924, when he burst upon that stage, he maintained a singularly consistent role as an ardent campaigner and champion of the under-dog, the ranker. Endowed with courage and great physical strength, he was able to perform feats which Byron would have envied, while his verse, like Byron's, carried the force and decisive edge of the man of action. The figure on the stage, who had cast himself so young for so romantic and heroic a part, was hardly more remarkable than the man in the wings himself, talking with a disarming modesty in those intervals between episodes of aggressive action, and devoting himself with humility to his art and to his friends.

Poetically Roy Campbell was the very opposite of Rilke; or it is perhaps truer to say that his type of courage was the very opposite of the type Rilke possessed. The one was active, positive, crusading; the other passive, receptive, enduring. Rilke did not recognize enemies, but to Roy Campbell, who saw everything as black or white, they were as dramatically necessary as the dragon was to Saint George. He was conscious, not only of an extreme poetic loneliness, but of an urgent sense of duty and of a need to daunt that Chimaera which represented to him the hesitant and the false.

Though born in South Africa, Roy Campbell was in the truest sense a European poet. His favourite country was Spain, which he knew better than any other. A friend of Lorca, he translated his plays and some of his poems; it was at the request of Lorca's parents that he decided to edit his works. His translations from Baudelaire and Rimbaud were, like those from Lorca, marked by his own accent, for his own poetic idiom was too characteristic to be lost in translation. Whether he translated from French, Spanish or Portuguese, he brought his own masculine equipment to the service of works of whose subtlety he was acutely aware. When he sacrificed subtlety for force the choice was his own, and deliberately made. He had the keenest appreciation of what was magical and untranslatable in poetry, as he showed when he talked about Lorca's short poems and the poems of Gongora. His translations from St John of the Cross, perhaps the finest he made, reveal an affinity of craftsmanship and of religious fervour. Accomplished though he was in the many fields of physical energy, he set the highest achievements of active life below the attainment of religious experience. Yet to the very end of his life both were linked in his imagination. A postcard showing the

Alcázar arrived from Toledo four days before his death, bearing these words: 'I am having a wonderful time convalescing in this heavenly place which means more than all the world to me, because it was here that the Devil was routed in 1936 – as never before or since.'

Alun Lewis

It is unusual to find in a poet killed before his thirtieth year a twofold promise such as the Welsh poet Alun Lewis possessed. Like Edward Thomas and Wilfred Owen in the war which preceded his own, he carried an invisible equipment in which a bitter awareness of the human condition and an intense compassion for people were welded together. He was a witness and an interpreter. He refused to be adopted by any clique. Arriving in India in the humility of friendship and service and the solitude of his own imagination, he expressed, as no-one else had done, the experience of those conditions which the common soldier could not communicate. The acute observation and penetration of his late prose and the sharp pathos of his verse were the outer facets of his own self-examination, a restless element which accompanied him everywhere. He knew already that if a poet listened to himself a nation would one day hear him; and he knew, too, that a prose writer could not lose himself too much in the activities of others.

John Milton

It's true that Shakespeare was a much better influence on Keats than Milton and that's why he gave up 'Hyperion'. But that isn't really a convincing argument against Latin artifice. Hopkins is influenced by Milton in quite a different way, and Housman again differently; both received Milton first-hand, one might say.

A Note on Heinrich Heine

Heine was born into the world with the nineteenth century. He was uncertain in which century he belonged, but he knew that he was born into the greatest age of poetry Germany had ever known. The poetry of Goethe was then at its highest power, and so was that of Hölderlin, though it is doubtful whether Heine ever read him; it is indeed most unlikely that he knew the greatest of Hölderlin's poems, written just when he was born. Goethe he did know, and when he was a young man he met him. He has written a memorable record of that encounter, describing Goethe's presence as the presence of a god. He says that his features, even in old age, were magnificent and might have served as a model to a Greek sculptor, and that his eyes were clear and still, like the eyes of Greek statues. He looked, he says, for the eagle at his shoulder.

Heine had as deep an admiration of Goethe as any German, yet he despised his egoism. If Goethe stands in

German poetry as the architect of conscious thought, Heine, attending always to the lightning of intuition, is the after-thought. In Heine's creed love is an absolute and dignity is an impostor. In his poetry he is capable of producing a wide range of effects, varying from the light and elusive music of his early lyrics and ballads to blank verse of a Shakespearian dignity and power. The dignity is, however, at the end of the poem, usually nudged by humour or translated into personal misery. The poems are made more elusive by the forced simplicity of their language and by Heine's use of the mask; they reveal themselves only in the cadence. Heine was deeply influenced by Shakespeare, but also by the poetry of the Middle Ages, by the Minnesangers and folk-poetry. There are trite and bad moments in the Buch der Lieder, but they belong to a pattern in which the mask has been used frequently and variously, and in which the secret has been kept. The most memorable lyrics of that book have become a part of folk-poetry, and they have an inexhaustible power of evocation, peculiar to Heine.

In 1856 Heine died in Paris, where he had spent half his life in exile from Germany. His wife was French, and he wrote freely in either language. There is a distinct French influence in his prose. He sympathized with the French, and in many passages he prophesied with great accuracy the tyranny of Prussia, and the wars it would bring to Europe. Although converted to Christianity when he was twenty-five, he was a champion of Jewry against racial persecution, and it was his courage and frankness which drove him into exile. He loved Germany, but the Germany of his time he did not love. He was doubly armed, for he had lightning wit and great affection. Both were, I think, misunderstood. When he died he had been almost completely paralysed for seven years, lying on what he used to call his 'mattress-grave'. His lyrical impulse never deserted him, and Théophile Gautier has described him upon his death-bed, still singing, almost inaudibly, beneath the sheet which was to be his shroud.

Vernon Watkins on Art and Artists

The Need of the Artist

What I have now to say was prompted by an exhibition which opened in Llanelly before the Eisteddfod and is now touring Wales. This exhibition is devoted to the work of Alfred Janes and Will Roberts. They are showing twenty-five paintings of each, covering approximately as many years. In either case you are looking at the work of half a lifetime.

There are many things to say about this exhibition of two fine Welsh painters who show such a marked contrast in their styles. I cannot, however, offer anything to the tide of current art criticism in the way of comment to satisfy those cormorants of curiosity who watch only the tide. For one thing, I have no professional qualification to speak. I am not myself a practising painter or draughtsman. I have seen my efforts in this direction surpassed by all my children except the youngest. I am pretty sure that in this subject I would fail, not only the eleven-plus examination, but the six- or seven-plus.

Yet there is a bond between all the arts of which I am deeply conscious. An artist is a man born with a need. This need is so urgent that it makes all activities return to it, as to a centre. The need is always accompanied by a gift, and the gift compels the artist to concentrate on it all his energy and attention. The demands of the imagination must be met: that is the need, and it is always in movement.

An artist, then, is someone whose life is incomplete and who is destined to complete it by his art. Does this incompleteness apply to society, does it apply to a town? A town without art is a dead town. A country aware of art is a living country. A city has no right to be remembered except for what a materialist would call its wasteful production.

Ezra Pound has said: 'Artists are the antennae of the race'. They are ahead of their time. Their heightened sensitivity already experiences what appears only gradually to their fellow men. They present what is already known, but with enhanced judgement; and they reveal what is unfamiliar, new aspects of form which are brought into the realm of common understanding. The works of a great master represent the need and the gift in their highest and most intense operation. Paradoxically such works may have been scarcely recognized in the lifetime of the artist. A town's richest treasure may be the works of a man who has this need and this gift, and who died penniless. Artists are the antennae of the race, and in the Past it usually took a generation, or more than one, to catch up with their genius. In poetry the recognition often comes later still, and a century may pass before the true need of the poet is reflected in his audience.

The excitement of painting, whether it is seen by the professional or by someone like me who cannot paint, is not only the excitement of the performance; it is also the excitement of detail and potential. To this excitement the fragment and the resolved work both belong.

Certainly in Wales to-day something extraordinary has happened. We are not living in a renaissance of painting, for the rich and varied works of visual art which Welsh painters are producing have no precedent in this country.

We are living, since approximately 1935, at the beginning of a tradition, and some of the paintings to be seen to-day may be among the first of its Old Masters. If we look back, say, to the beginning of this century, we find the example of Innes, a Llanelly man, whose sensitive nature gave him a reaction to landscape which made his paintings distinctly his own; and we have the very considerable example of Augustus John. What we do not have is a precedent for the kind of painting that is being produced by the best Welsh artists to-day, works of professional excellence whose richness and scope and far-reaching experiment could not have been foreseen.

The sudden presentation of a wide range of new work by gifted artists has been accompanied by a keener awareness of art than ever existed in Wales before, an awareness which the Arts Council, by sponsoring exhibitions, has been at pains to foster. The teaching of art has become much more expert and more widely diffused. People's interest is no longer retrospective alone; it is also directed, probably more than ever before in this country, to contemporary achievement, to what is being produced. Among a great many people visual art has become a part of life, and they have gained access to art through the present day's assimilation of the ages. It is now up to them to feel their way back, and again forward.

I must return to the two artists of this exhibition. I was not fortunate enough to meet Will Roberts as early as Alfred Janes. I knew many of his paintings and would quickly recognize them before I met the man. He is concerned with everyday life, with the way people live and work, or do not work. He is able to give dignity to the casual scene, and make it memorable. Landscape and figure are subordinated to a mood. He is a warm painter, and he understands the vibrations of intimate life, whether the scene is a farm or a country road or a room where people are talking or going to sleep. It is the ephemeral moment he records, in a forceful and simple way. He has evolved his own recognizable world, and he communicates it at once.

All art is unpredictable, and a painter's own development is unpredictable, too. When I first met Alfred Janes in 1935 he was absorbed in a certain kind of still life. He had developed a particularly brilliant method of handling the geometric patterns of fish and fruit in a kind of musical order. There are examples of this early style among this exhibition's twenty-five paintings. He told me at this time that perhaps the greatest influence on his painting was the Double Violin Concerto of Bach. His method was so painstaking that he would spend hundreds of hours, perhaps six months, on the same canvas; and his patience became a by-word among his friends. Even in 1946 Dylan Thomas was writing to me in a letter: 'How is that blizzardly painter, that lightning artist, that prodigal canvas-stacker? Has he reached the next finbone of the fish he was dashing off before the war?' Between those early still-life paintings and the magnificent abstracts, that are not really abstracts, which are his most recent work, there is a sustained history of concentration and self-renewal in this artist. He has never become smug or lost his urge to experiment. Dylan Thomas would be amazed at the profusion of paintings that have emerged from these successive styles. In each stage of Alfred Janes' development there is an extraordinary meticulousness and mastery, at once recognizable as his own.

What is the bond between these two artists, who are so contrasted in their styles? It is complete integrity, complete honesty. Neither is pompous. If an artist becomes pompous, it always spoils his work. If the gift outruns the need, he becomes a virtuoso, he loses the thread of concentration and gives himself over to display. Integrity is at the root of all great art, at the source of what is eternally fresh, eternally beginning. In every true master the need of the imagination is the first thing before him.

The bond between all artists is the recognition of the incompleteness, even the barrenness, of life without art. I am not saying that the need or the ability to create art is the highest and most indispensable gift of man: charity is clearly that. But I do say that art is man's most exhilarating, as well as his most searching, activity.

There are Welsh artists now unmatched by any others in their particular medium; their integrity has reached a point where comparison ceases to be relevant. The force and the poetry of colour in Ceri Richards belong to this pure, unrivalled air; and there is a coherence of vision in all that David Jones touches, whether in language or design, painting or drawing, that sets him apart. There are many others.

The need of the artist is, as I have said, in movement, and it is impossible to define a school of Welsh painting, to set national limits. For what is a national artist? In order to see the paintings of Will Roberts and Alfred Janes I travelled down from Swansea to Llanelly. A national artist could only make that journey slowly, and with a great many changes. He would have to see, not only European art, but that art of Asia, Africa and America. He could not arrive without considering for a long time the paintings of the Lascaux caves. In all the arts we look to ancient examples; all achievement has a reference to what has gone before. The history of art is not only the history of civilisations, but on a deeper level the history of man's sensibility. What was valid in remote times as an aesthetic marvel is valid now, and the excitement then experienced is our excitement. Art is a spring that is never dry. It is the ancestral wonder of art, from its first beginnings, in those masterpieces of so many ages, which throws the paintings on these walls into relief.

Vernon Watkins July-August 1962

Note on David Jones

Certain artists fall into a period which reflects an age or a fashion, and their excellence is in a sense historical. Others use history as a tool in their hands and so manipulate it that their work extends far beyond the province of their age and becomes applicable to all ages. The work of David Jones belongs to the second category. The history of one man's experience, if intensely recorded, contains the history of the race.

Wales is to-day honouring an artist who has already honoured her. Half Welsh by birth, David Jones has exhibited in his two great books 'In Parenthesis' and 'The Anathemata' a technique where power and delicacy serve each other, and, by strictness of cadence, obey a controlling vision. One property of this vision is to see as contemporary what is ancient and to see as ancient what is before his eyes. It is a religious vision projecting a symbolic art, and through this art, whether in literature, painting or drawing, shines his love of man and of all that is precious to him, and a particular love of Wales and these islands drawn from the roots of earliest customs and ways of living.

David Jones was already famous in his native art of painting and drawing before he began as a writer. Now he has achieved world-wide distinction in two arts, and there are few such examples in Britain before him. Blake is one. Blake said: 'Everything that lives is holy'. He might also have said what David Jones wrote in 'The Tutelar of the Place' a few years ago, with his eyes fixed on the removal of things and places whose existence and tradition seemed sacred to him: 'Save us from the men who plan.'

Exuberance

'Energy is eternal delight' (Blake). Vernon Watkins on his friend Ceri Richards seems to bear this out.

In writing about Ceri Richards I am overwhelmed by a rush of images before I begin. They all belong to an unmistakable idiom, a clenched source of power. It is as though he had seized the forces of nature and reconstituted them in his own person.

Baudelaire, who wrote of Delacroix: '*Les couleurs pensent*', might say today of Ceri Richards: '*Les couleurs chantent*'. The violence of these paintings is in their stillness: their silence holds an inherent music. Statements may adorn the magic of the surface, but they cannot interfere with the stubborn course of genius.

Before the Welsh painter set out, he was already an accomplished musician. From the first, his pictures evoked, through the dazzling virtuosity of their technique, the intimacy of music. It dominated the 'Homage to Beethoven' paintings of the early fifties, just as it is found in the marvellous variations on Debussy's '*Le Poisson d'Or*' and '*La Cathédrale Engloutie*'.

One characteristic of this artist is his fidelity to particular themes. Trafalgar Square, an old Beekeeper, the Rape of the Sabines and the Lion Hunt were images to which he returned. And Debussy's music was a starting-point for a sea voyage which has unloaded perhaps the deepest treasures of his imagination so far, a voyage of many years in which the extraordinary resources of the painter's inner vision were beckoned forth by the music. The contracted poise and animation of the many early pianist variations yield here to the mass and reverberation, under striped and scored surfaces, of architectural echoes and organ stops submerged in the mystery of the sea.

No less compelling to his imagination has been the poetry of Dylan Thomas, whose early poem 'The Force that Through the Green Fuse Drives the Flower' was the theme of several paintings made in 1945; but not until a month before the poet died did they meet. After his death Ceri Richards handled the imagery of the later poetry with wonderful effect. The series of pen and wash designs for the drop cloth of the Globe Theatre Memorial Recital 'Homage to Dylan Thomas' in 1954 capture with terrifying clarity the shrouded body caught between heron and owl, or the living boy racing from sight. These are in no sense illustrations, but independent creations. Both poet and painter are Welsh, and their affinity rests also in a sensuous response to the created world and to the predicament of man. The same tension is revealed in paintings based on the poem 'Do Not Go Gentle Into That Good Night'.

The sustained development of an artist is no accident. Gaiety, wit, joy and exuberance, all make Ceri Richards' work robust. It is in his nature to exult rather than be disillusioned, to define strength rather than elegance, and to stamp the fragile and the ephemeral with permanence. Both he and Dylan Thomas share the vision of Blake. Both know that Minute Particulars, rather than any generalized view of the world, are the source of organic strength. The relief constructions of the thirties belong much more to Ceri Richards' development than to any climate of taste. This is true of all his productions. Poetry and music are frequently used as an imaginative base for releasing his own energies, in swirling movement and concentrated speed, or in the falling movement and dilated wonder of the paintings from my poem 'Music of Colours – White Blossom.' He is a European painter whose violence and controlled delicacy are Welsh gifts. At the 1962 Venice Biennale people from all over the world were astonished by his subtle harnessing of lyric mobility to sculptural strength, of exhilaration to profound feeling, of movement to repose.

The line itself sings, less from appreciation than from praise. Where does sensuousness end and thought begin, when both give such immediate pleasure, and project so instantly the mystery at the heart of painting, poetry and music? And who better understands tragedy than one who has joy at his fingertips?

In my poem 'The Forge of the Solstice' I called him to mind with two other Welsh painters, David Jones and Alfred Janes, and in the second verse tried to express one aspect of his work:

Another, curbing vigour on his page
To movement, makes the abounding life his own
And rhythmic finds in a discordant age,
Singing like living fountains sprung from stone
Those unifying harmonies of line.

In Defence of Sound

If in this age there is to be an artistic revival, it is likely to come unobserved. If something so serious happens it will happen against the current of contemporary taste. Least of all will it be noticed by the television camera. The appetite of the television camera is the appetite of curiosity, and it is fed by the topical, at its most energetic by the active moment in time, at its most relaxed by extensive glimpses into people's lives. The supreme achievements of active life, the winning of a historic race or the performance of a unique experiment, may be caught by the television camera, and their excitement remains. Millions may now witness a single memorable event and the moment of its climax. They do, however, play a passive part, and such moments are rare. The staple food of this whale of an audience is too small for the naked eye.

There remains the audience for sound. These are more likely to detect what is new and will one day be ancient without being old. In artistic performance, although they lose the positions of the players, they are saved many embarrassments. They can build the scene for themselves and attend to what is spoken. When words are sung they do not have to see the singer's mouth, when notes are played they need lose nothing of the music for the sake of the musician's hands. They need not observe a bad actor's declamatory gestures or the shuffling of a cramped chorus. There is, in fact, without a producer of genius, a better chance of presenting Greek drama through sound radio than through any other medium. The true theatre is in the mind's eye, and the true action of the theatre springs from solitude and darkness. Certainly, in tragedy and comedy, actors on the stage may make an unforgettable impression, but the unity of the play is sometimes consumed by their own virtuosity, and there are certain No plays for which the Japanese bend their heads; similarly such a play as Yeats' 'The Words upon the Window-Pane', or 'Purgatory', may be produced more powerfully through sound radio than ever on stage.

In sport, in pageantry and ceremonial, in showing countries and people's faces, migrating birds and all types of creation, television has something to give. But from art it always takes away. The moving photograph, which makes no demands on the imagination of the beholder but only on his curiosity, is sufficient for television. The cameras do not want art; in their triumphant progress from one scene to another they really have no time for it. They pause to present plays, but apologetically, for they are aware of their own discomfort. Their habit is naturalistic; and although nature follows art, it does not stay with it. Television is interested in the faces of artists, and faces are always interesting. But art is interesting, too, and art does not need cameras.

Vernon Watkins October 31st 1958

Afterword

by Gwen Watkins

Some years after Vernon's death, I was asked to read and discuss a selection of his poems to a Ladies' literary Society. Afterwards, an old lady came up to me and said in a soft voice, 'But what was he like as a human being?'

I foresaw that this was going to take some time, so we sat on a bench (the meeting was, appropriately, in a chapel – the very chapel, in fact, where Dylan Thomas had spent so many Sunday afternoons, longing to be down on the Mumbles seashore) and I told the old lady that Vernon had been a devoted husband, a loving father who had played games with his children, helped them with their homework, read to them and been read to by them; that he worked in a very busy bank, in those days on Saturday mornings too, that he left home before 8.30 and was seldom back before 6p.m. That he loved swimming, walking in Gower, catching prawns and lobsters and occasionally fish, that he was a passionate sportsman who played hockey and cricket and watched Glamorgan whenever they played at St Helen's, that he had many friends whom he saw as often as he could and that he listened to a great deal of classical music.

'And you may not know,' I said 'that he published, besides seven books of poems and a verse play, two books of translations, and many other translations from French, German, Italian, Spanish and indeed from Hungarian; also from Latin as well. I went on remorselessly, 'He taught in universities at Swansea and Seattle, and gave talks all over Britain, and in France and America.' 'My goodness,' said the old lady feebly. 'Yes, and after his death, we found piles and piles of papers, unfinished poems, and, surprisingly, quite a lot of prose articles.' 'Were there any stories?' she asked hopefully. 'No, indeed,' I said. 'They were all about poets, poetry and how to write poetry; and he seemed to know where poetry came from!' Like the Queen of Sheba, there was no spirit left in the old lady. 'My, my,' she murmured feebly; but then she came back with a saying which I have often thought about since. 'It seems as though,' she said, 'he must have been a lot different from all the rest of us.' Other people thought so, all his life. In the memorial volume published after his death, his close friend Michael Hamburger calls him 'one of the most admirable and lovable of men'; James Laughlin, his American publisher, calls him 'just, plainly, such a loveable person.' Glyn Jones describes him as 'one of the kindest of men', and Hugo Williams, a much younger man with whom he once carried out a tour reading poems at different places along the route, was both amused and delighted by his 'kind of zany chivalry which made people love him'. At a grand tea, he would cheerfully offer round from a brown paper bag unshelled prawns which he had caught that morning, or with one prong of his silver cake-knife send fragments of meringue speeding to all corners of the room. Incidents such as these would have disconcerted a less humble man, but Vernon accepted them as part of his life. What he could never accept was his complete inability to perform simple practical actions such as mending a fuse, putting a fan-belt on a vacuum cleaner, removing screws from any small object without instantly losing them.

These failures would drive him into acts of furious rage such as upending and violently shaking a grandmother clock to make it chime, or battering to death an oil-stove from which he had failed to remove a worn-out wick. With infinite patience he would wait months or even years for a poem to be perfect, but he could never wait three minutes for a bus to arrive, or a train to start.

What powered, drove and exalted him, what was 'Felt in the blood, and felt along the heart,' as Wordsworth put it, was poetry; his own and that of other poets. It gave him almost the same sense of satisfaction to discover a fine poem by an unknown writer as to complete a poem of his own; as for the great poets of Britain, France and Germany they were like breathing to him. I never mentioned or quoted a poet whom he did not know and whom he could not quote from: but he did not care for anthologies. He felt that one should devote one's whole attention to the work of one poet at a time without being distracted by the work of another. He believed that all great art was dictated or suggested by higher powers (or Powers) than those of humanity; and since he was mainly a lyric poet, the immortal with whom he had most dealings was the Muse of Lyric verse.

Poets through the ages, from Virgil to Milton have believed in and invoked the favour of the Muses. Milton said that in old age he could command the Muse to do whatever he wanted. Vernon was not so fortunate; he found his particular Lady difficult to deal with. Sometimes her communications would sound like a very faint telephone call, with many words or lines inaudible, so that the poet had to labour to find the missing words – and only the right words would do. Sometimes she would neglect him for weeks or months at a time, sometimes require his attention when he was particularly busy. There seemed no way to ensure her undivided attention. 'It's the emotions of girls that I simply don't understand', he grumbled to Philip Larkin; and as he aged he gave up trying to understand this particular Girl, but simply acquiesced in her erratic behaviour. If she neglected him, he turned to translation or comic verse; if he was too busy to attend to her demands, she simply had to wait.

Vernon Watkins wrote more about poets and about the writing of poetry than any poet before or after Wordsworth. His book 'Affinities' consists almost entirely of poems on these subjects. He thought that Dylan Thomas and he would live into old age, their poems 'moving', he said, 'like Swedenborg's angels, towards the dayspring of their youth.' It was not to be. Neither poet lived into old age. Dylan Thomas wrote in 1951 'the joy and function of poetry is, and was, the celebration of man, which is also the celebration of God.' I think Vernon Watkins would have agreed; except that he might have said, 'The joy and function of poetry is, and was, the celebration of God, which is also the celebration of man.'

Gwen Watkins 2013

On the Photograph with Philip Larkin

Did poets ever look more dull
Than these two, just arrived from Hull?
Better had they been left in hiding
Than brought to beam on every Riding.
Lost property with none to claim them,
My painful duty is to name them:
The dexter Watkins, Larkin sinister,
At Beverley, quite near the Minster.
Since bless relaxes and damn braces
And there's no prize for funny faces,
No Nobel Prize or rich annuity
To breed a pension for fatuity
(Leeds' kindly lights would fail the test
And Sheffield's spade-beard give them best),
I'll set them up without apology
As neighbours to the next anthology,
Stretching its life upon the rack
While woodworms wonder and turn back.

Acknowledgements

The editors wish to thank:

Katie Bowman for her work typing and transcribing the mass of vintage manuscripts she was presented with.

Gareth Watkins for providing a rich choice of photographs and all the Watkins, young and older who helped Gwen in her battle with the computer.

Carys and all at Parthian for all their help support and enthusiasm for the book.

Baron Williams of Oystermouth – Dr Rowan Williams for his enthusiasm and contribution

And Jeff offers humble gratitude to his wife Elizabeth and his family for putting up with his excesses.

Index